Despair, fatigue, and frustration ˋ ministry. How does one not onl preacher when there is little aftᵢ ... growth? Here is a book that gives advice and inspiration for preachers who need encouragement to stay true to their calling to preach the Word (2 Tim. 4:1).

Joe Barnard
Founder of Cross Training Ministries

This book was birthed in the crucible of criticism, disappointment and the continuing conviction that if we are faithful to the Scriptures our labor is never in vain. This is not a theoretical book written about how to preach but rather an honest account of preaching when you'd rather quit; preaching when you are constantly criticized and when some people would prefer if you'd just leave the church.

From the Bible, and from examples drawn from Church history, as well as their personal experiences, these authors encouraged my own heart. If the fire in your heart is burning low, this is the book that will help reignite the gift God has given you to be a faithful preacher, no matter the cost.

Erwin W. Lutzer
Pastor Emeritus, The Moody Church, Chicago

What brings profound change to a congregation? A dynamic preacher? A strategic move to a better location? Better music? No, the change agent for a congregation is the same as it is for the individual: the faithful preaching—week in and week out—of God's inspired, inerrant Word. This unique book is a reminder of the fundamental reality. It seems I have read enough books on preaching to populate a small book store, but never one like this. Both authors have served as faithful preachers in a revitalizing context for many years and have long practiced the things they write about here. Read it and be reminded (and instructed) that the power of God for transformation—for the church—lies in what the apostle Paul calls 'the foolishness of preaching'.

Jeff Robinson
Lead Pastor, Christ Fellowship Church of Louisville, Kentucky, and Senior Editor, The Gospel Coalition

There is sufficient simple biblical realism in this volume to make it widely applicable. Both authors have faced particular battles in different difficult contexts, and both seek to filter that experience through the grid of Scripture to give counsels and encouragements for those seeking to revitalise troubled or stubborn churches in accordance with the Word of God. Even more settled pastors in more solid churches will find much to stimulate and to instruct in this helpful and accessible volume.

Jeremy Walker
Pastor, Maidenbower Baptist Church, UK

I believe my good friend, Brian Croft, and his co-author James Carroll, have given a treasure to the church in this book! Every pastor needs to read this book, embrace it, and let it speak to them about how they can take their preaching up a notch. Read it. Then let it read you. May God use it to bring a revival of gospel preaching in Bible-believing churches in North America.

Mark Clifton
Director of Replanting and Revitalization
North American Mission Board

BRIAN CROFT &
JAMES B. CARROLL
FOREWORD BY MARK CLIFTON

FACING
SNARLS&
SCOWLS

PREACHING THROUGH
HOSTILITY, APATHY, AND ADVERSITY
IN CHURCH REVITALIZATION

CHRISTIAN
FOCUS

Copyright © Brian Croft and James B. Carroll 2019

paperback ISBN 978-1-5271-0382-5
epub ISBN 978-1-5271-0400-6
mobi ISBN 978-1-5271-0401-3

First published in 2019
by
Christian Focus Publications Ltd,
Geanies House, Fearn, Ross-shire,
IV20 1TW, Scotland
www.christianfocus.com

with

Practical Shepherding, Inc
P.O. Box 21806
Louisville, Kentucky 40221, USA

www.practicalshepherding.com

A CIP catalogue record for this book is available
from the British Library.

Cover design by Tom Barnard

Printed and bound by
Bell & Bain, Glasgow.

Contents

Foreword 7

Preface 11

Introduction 15

Part 1: You are in Good Company

1. Enduring Preachers in the Bible 25

2. Enduring Preachers in Church History 41

**Part 2: Do not Give them a Good Reason to
Hate Your Preaching**

3. Bad Preaching Deserves Rebuke 59

4. Basics in Expository Preaching 73

5. Faithful Preaching Over the Long-term 87

Part 3: Preaching with Your Feet to the Fire

6. Preaching through Hostility 103

7. Preaching through Apathy 117

8. Preaching through Adversity 133

Conclusion 151

Acknowledgements...157

Dedication

To the ones who know our struggles to persevere
through snarls and scowls best,
our wives and best friends, Cara and Mikila.
Your partnership on this journey is an
inexpressible joy.
Thank you and we love you.

FOREWORD

You see them everywhere. Some have been turned into coffee shops. Others have been flipped into restaurants and condominiums. Many, many others have been completely torn down, and now office buildings or parking lots sit in their places.

They're churches. Once thriving places of worship in communities all around North America. They proclaimed the gospel boldly and unapologetically in all kinds of communities big and small. They made disciples who made disciples. They sent out preachers and missionaries to every corner of the world. But today these churches sit empty – monuments to a different era.

There is a crisis of dying churches in North America. Most experts estimate that 4,000 churches close their doors every single year. I don't believe there is anything about a church's death that brings glory to God. Nothing about a dead church that proclaims: 'Our God is great and His gospel is powerful.'

So why do these churches die? Though many of them sit in urban areas where new people come in daily, still these churches die. Though the remaining members may continue to participate in a full array of activities and plug along year after year, still these churches move toward death. Many of these churches continue to disconnect from their community as they trade the comfort of the familiar for the power of the gospel.

In my role as the director of replanting and revitalization for the North American Mission Board, of the Southern Baptist Convention, I see countless examples of churches well located among unreached neighbors that slowly slide toward eventual closure. Of course, these churches close their doors for many reasons, but it's the lack of consistent biblical preaching that leads the way to decline. But some of you may say, 'Wait! Our church and our pastor believe the Bible and we preach from it every week.' No doubt that may be true. But is it the kind of consistent, rightly dividing of the Word of God that will cause church members to forgo their own comfort and sacrificially live and give to reach the community around them?

It's easy to get caught up in a million other things that people say can revive a dying church. Some people want to change the music. Others will tell you that you need a new logo and a new name. Others want you to remove the pews and put in folding chairs. But let me be very clear. I've seen God turn around churches in every corner of North America. I've seen Him do miracles that I would never have believed unless I saw them with my own eyes. I've never once seen God change a church because of the music. I've never once seen Him bring revival because of a logo or a new name. I've never seen Him bring new life when a church takes the pews out. Those things and many others may take place as the church comes back to life but they are the effect of new life and not the cause.

Only biblical preaching can make dead men come back to life. And only biblical preaching can bring a dead church back to life. But the sad truth is, most people don't even know what biblical preaching is and what its purpose is. Until we understand the nature of biblical preaching and how God uses it to bring life to dying churches, our churches won't become the models of gospel transformation He intends them to become.

That's why I believe my good friend, Brian Croft, and his co-author James Carroll, have given a treasure to the church in this book! Every pastor needs to read this book, embrace it, and let it speak to them about how they can take their preaching up a notch. When the Apostle Paul urges young Timothy to stay committed to the church at Ephesus despite all of its issues, he reminded him to teach good doctrine. Paul knew nothing else young Timothy did mattered more for the health of his church than the faithful preaching of sound doctrine. It's the consistent preaching of God's Word that the Holy Spirit will use to change the minds and hearts of people. It's the consistent preaching of God's Word that will help people love Jesus more. Jesus has a plan for every dying church. Our people will understand the plan when they know Jesus better.

That'll happen when they get consistent biblical preaching. That's why I'm thankful for *Facing Snarls and Scowls*. A book like this has never been more needed in the history of the church in North America.

Read it. Then let it read you. May God use it to bring a revival of gospel preaching in Bible-believing churches in North America.

Mark Clifton
Director of Replanting and Revitalization
North American Mission Board
January 2019

Preface

'The world doesn't need another preaching book.'

At least, that was my initial response when James first proposed the idea for this book. There is this encouraging recovery and focus as of late on biblical preaching. As a result, several strong and helpful books about preaching have been released in the last decade. So I didn't see the need. But James still insisted I would want to hear his idea. James is a good friend, wise, thoughtful, and has great ideas. So, I listened. Before my cup of coffee was gone, he had me hooked. Here's why.

There are many strong books on preaching, but there are very few books in regard to preaching in a church revitalization context. In fact, I'm convinced there's nothing like the book you hold in your hands. Let's face it. The hard work of church revitalization is a unique experience and battle ground. Both James and I had been doing the pastoral work of church revitalization before it became the trendy topic it is, especially among Southern Baptists. Consequently, we are encouraged by the flood of solid resources for church revitalization that has emerged in the last five years, but most of these resources focus on different philosophies and strategies to gain traction in the work. Few still break down the most significant roles that revitalization pastors need to engage in to be productive and faithful in this work.

Arguably, biblical preaching is one of the most important tools in the hand of the Chief Shepherd as He seeks to breathe life back into struggling, dying churches. It is by the Word of God through the Spirit of God that true, lasting life is restored. Ground zero for this work is found at the foot of the pulpit every Sunday. This is true in any church. And yet, the unique challenges found in church revitalization make this all the truer and more essential.

What are those unique challenges? In my church, I discovered not just a tough room in which to preach, but a hostile room filled with snarls and scowls. James found a Sunday morning crowd apathetic to biblical preaching as a result of a deeply embedded pragmatism in his church. We both experienced adversities that are in some form quite certain for every revitalization pastor. As I have had the privilege to work with many pastors immersed in church revitalization, our experiences are quite common. A persevering preaching ministry in the midst of some form of hostility, apathy, and adversity becomes the litmus test to how much can one man endure as he seeks to revitalize a church.

Therefore, the aim of this book is twofold. First, we want the reader to know hostility, apathy, and adversity is 'par for the course' if one sets out to do the work of church revitalization. You will not be the exception. A commitment to biblical, expository preaching will only make these struggles even more certain for the pastor who seeks to preach God's Word faithfully as Paul commanded Timothy (2 Tim. 4:1-5). Second, it is possible, by the grace of God, to endure, remain steadfast, and see the ship of a dying church turn in time. When it does, there is no sweeter place for a pastor to preach than a church with faces once peppered with snarls and scowls now transformed to receive God's Word preached with conviction, eagerness, and tears of joy.

Brian Croft
October 2018

INTRODUCTION

A Call to Perseverance

On the spectrum between cynical and gullible, I (James) lean toward the former. I'm likely to respond, 'there's no way!' when I hear an improbable story or to research incredible facts before believing them and certainly before repeating them to others. I assume people embellish their stories, shade the narrative, or engage in creative retelling to make it sound more compelling. It's not that people are maliciously lying; it's that the storytelling is an invigorating experience and most people get caught up in the moment. Perhaps it's a fault, but I just don't buy much of what is sold as truth, especially when it's a movie or book that is 'based on a true story'.

If you've heard the story of Louis Zamperini's life, you can imagine how I responded to it. I was completely unaware of him until I picked up his biography, *Unbroken: A World War II Story of Survival, Resilience, and Redemption*, written by Laura Hillenbrand a few years ago. I couldn't stop reading because the story is so moving and at the same time, un-be-liev-a-ble. So I did what I normally do in that situation, I scoured the internet for book reviews and for additional sources of information about Zamperini to verify what I'd read. From everything I could find, Hillenbrand accurately recounted the epic tale of endurance.

One reviewer called the story 'one of the most remarkable – and appalling – to emerge' from a war that has produced dozens of compelling stories. Zamperini enlisted in the United States Army Air Corps in 1941 and was stationed in the south Pacific as a bombardier. While on a mission searching for a lost bomber, his plane crashed killing eight of the eleven men onboard. After surviving the crash, Zamperini and two others drifted on two small rafts in the open ocean for more than a month and a half. During that time, they drank only small amounts of rainwater and ate small fish and birds that landed on their raft. They fended off numerous shark attacks, nearly capsized in a storm, and were strafed multiple times by Japanese bombers. One of the three men died on the thirty-third day of the ordeal.

After forty-seven days, Zamperini and the other man, Russell Phillips, landed in the Marshall Islands, but their story of survival was just beginning. Immediately captured by the Japanese, they were held in torturous POW camps for the next two years. Zamperini endured horrific mental and physical abuse throughout his imprisonment and unconscionable torment at the hands of one of Japan's most notorious war criminals, Mutsuhiro 'The Bird' Watanabe. When the war came to an end, he was released in August 1945 and returned home to a hero's welcome.

As you can imagine, he struggled to resume life in the U.S., suffering with flashbacks of his torture and nightmares, often drinking heavily in an attempt to forget the past. But in 1949, at the urging of his wife, he attended a Billy Graham crusade in Los Angeles and was transformed by the gospel of Christ. He found spiritual renewal and healing that reshaped his life and produced the fruit of forgiveness, even for those who had mistreated him so severely as a prisoner of war.

From a purely human perspective, Zamperini's story inspires and uplifts. How can a man endure this much suffering? Yet from a Christian worldview, we understand it as much more than a tale of human survival. It's a testimony to the grace and power of God. No person could endure the war, shipwreck, or cruel imprisonment without God's sustaining grace. Even more, no one could walk that road and come to the point of forgiveness without God's transforming grace. The body would collapse, the mind would fail, and the heart would grow increasingly bitter. It's a great story, but not humanly possible. No one could emerge from that suffering to enjoy mental and spiritual peace for decades afterward. That is, no one could without the power of God. So we give the credit to the God who saved Louis, from World War II and then rescued him from something worse than a POW camp: the penalty and power of sin. Again, from every angle, this story is unbelievable.

But if we're honest, Zamperini's story is as far away as it is fascinating. At no point in reading it did I think I could replicate it. I can't imagine spending one night on the open ocean, spending one day in a POW camp, or spending one minute on the sharp side of an executioner's sword. His story might make the hair on my neck stand up, but it doesn't make me think I could walk in his shoes. I love the story, but it is more likely to embarrass me than it is to motivate me. It makes me want to look in the mirror and say, 'Hey cry baby, until they rip out your fingernails, you need to quit whining.' The harrowing tale illustrates perseverance in a way that only highlights my weakness.

It might seem odd, but we open the book with the extraordinary story of Louis Zamperini because of the contrasts and comparisons to our primary theme: perseverance in preaching. First, his story is nothing like ours in a variety of ways. We (a couple of pastors) are ill-equipped to prepare you for survival in a life raft or in a prison camp. Our keyboard fingers look more like they've had a manicure than done manual labor. (Just so we're clear, I've never had a manicure!) Most years we suffer more paper cuts on our hands than work blisters. Our neck and back pain have more to do with the way we rest our arms on the mousepad than from lifting, carrying, or swinging a heavy tool. We have little to nothing in common with Louis from a physical standpoint.

Yet despite the obvious differences, his story compares well with what we're called to do in pastoral ministry. As a pastor you probably won't float in a raft until you nearly starve to death, but you might find yourself adrift amid the tumultuous waters of financial stress, wondering how you'll feed your family. You probably won't face torturers who try to break you physically, mentally, and emotionally, but you will suffer the physical effects of the emotional and mental weight of ministry burdens. And your leadership efforts will, at times, churn the waters within a local congregation and draw predators to the surface.

You probably won't face all manner of insults ... oh wait ... you likely will face that one. You probably won't face constant threats on your life, but you will be attacked. At times these assaults will come from those in obvious opposition to you and your leadership, but at other times, they'll arrive in the form of friends. The experiences are miles apart, but they correlate.

Take nothing away from Louis and his remarkable story, but endurance is as necessary for pastors as it is for POWs. I'm not diminishing the gravity of what he faced or presuming to know what he suffered, but pastoral ministry is not for the faint of heart. Surviving four decades in pastoral ministry is just as miraculous as surviving four years in a prison camp. Neither is humanly possible; both require God's grace and power. One could even argue that surviving in ministry is more remarkable because the battle behind it is supernatural and not natural. I'm not going to argue this with a POW, but I think you get the point. This book grows out of our burden for pastors to persevere in pulpit ministry and finish their race.

Before we move on, however, we need to state an important point. We're keenly aware that many lazy men have 'retired' from pastoral ministry. We've served with sloths who found the pastorate to be a comfortable place to hide. In fact, we have faced the temptation ourselves and have not stewarded every day perfectly. Pastors generally enjoy a good deal of freedom as ministry demands play give and take. The needs for pastoral care take by coming at inconvenient times and requiring personal sacrifice. Yet, the needs also give liberty because they are not constant. Inasmuch as ministry commandeers more than its share of evenings and weekends, it often repays with autonomy and flexibility on weekdays. Thus, we can appear plenty busy while frittering away Tuesday mornings and Thursday afternoons. Even more, we know that experienced pastors can talk for thirty-plus minutes about a given passage without proper study. Faithful stewardship requires more than activity; it requires our best.

We raise this fact from the outset to clarify that perseverance in preaching is not merely delivering some sort of spiritual talk once a week for decades. Rather, it's faithfully laboring for hours in the study, then passionately and accurately proclaiming God's Word from the pulpit week after week. The persevering pastor must avoid failure at both ends of the spectrum. He mustn't succumb to the burdens and abandon his post. Nor should he allow the burdens to weary him to the point that he continues without zeal and simply 'mails it in.' Our goal in writing is to strengthen pastors to persevere – not merely persist – in preaching. Perseverance is not less than longevity, but it certainly is more.

A Call to Persevere

These difficulties in pastoral ministry combine to call for a word that will encourage and equip a generation of pastors to labor with endurance in all fields, but especially in the difficult ones of church revitalization. Thus, we've teamed up to write out of the deep convictions regarding preaching, a deep love for pastors, and firsthand experience with this struggle. God's Word is often not very popular, and endurance in ministry is not humanly possible. Like many pastors, we know something of Isaiah's experience of preaching to deaf ears in seasons of stagnation and even decline. We can empathize with Paul's description of his ministry in Macedonia: 'fighting without and fear within.'

In the spirit of old school Baptist preachers, we want to encourage and challenge you with three points. First, the trials associated with preaching ministry are not new. Throughout the scriptures and church history, faithful preachers have labored under the weight of hostility, apathy, and adversity. We use these three categories because they encompass most specific circumstances in one way or another. Hostility refers to aggression toward God, His Word, and/or the preacher. Apathy refers to indifference toward God, His Word, and/or preaching. Adversity refers to a wide variety of crises that affect the preacher, including everything from personal and family burdens to church-related emergencies to community catastrophes.

Second, you might be part of the problem. While this book is certainly not a comprehensive treatment of the subject, we'll outline the basics of expository preaching and warn you about the most immediate dangers to it. It doesn't honor God to preach lousy sermons and blame the people for disliking it. Instead, the preacher ought to labor faithfully in the study working hard to craft and deliver sermons that expose the meaning of a biblical text and make relevant application to the people.

Finally, you're not alone. Once again, we preach through hostility, apathy, and adversity. We haven't faced every trial or circumstance, but we've preached to blank stares, dodged grenades from opponents, taken friendly fire, and persisted amid internal strife. We'll share our personal stories praying that God will give you hope and courage to keep pressing forward.

Imagine your average Monday morning. How would you describe your state of mind? Feel like you're lying in a raft in the middle of the ocean clinging to life? Did you barely manage to escape the strafing by the enemy and the 'friendly fire' yesterday? Feel like their prepping for another attack? Do you feel alone? On an island surrounded by people, but without a friend? Feel like a complete failure? Disappointed in yourself because of yet another subpar sermon? Do you feel beaten and battered? Overwhelmed with stress that has nothing to do with the previous day?

Regardless of your state of mind, perseverance is possible because it is a Holy Spirit-empowered, God-honoring, Christ-exalting work. The Lord of Sunday is still the Lord on Monday. Your circumstance has come by His gracious and sovereign hand and these trials are for His purpose in you. He is building His Church and making you blameless at the same time. Don't lose hope, for the One who has called you is faithful, and He will surely do it.

PART 1

YOU ARE IN GOOD COMPANY

1

ENDURING PREACHERS IN THE BIBLE

The Word of Faith movement and the related prosperity gospel are plagues on twenty-first century Christianity. They alter the truth of Scripture, disarm the gospel of its power, weaken genuine disciples, and devastate churches. The swath of destruction stretches throughout America and around the world leaving outwardly-identifying, but biblically-unrecognizable Christians. Millions of self-identifying Christians attend churches propagating some form of these lies. On a superficial level, the churches look the same – the cross is prominently displayed, Jesus is regularly mentioned, the Bible is frequently referenced – yet at the core they are irreconcilably different. What masquerades as a living form of the faith once for all delivered to the saints is, in reality, a casket-ready-corpse: dead on the inside and dressed up to look alive.

This brand of false teaching threatens to shipwreck historically strong churches because of its insidious half-truths. One of the most powerful lessons from Genesis 3 emerges from the serpent's ability to convince Eve and then

Adam to disobey God's clear directive by misquoting Him. From Eden onward, the adversary's most sinister plots concoct subtle poisons from the deep well of distortion. Frontal assaults on truth usually have some effect, but they pale in comparison to what chicanery from within or attacks from the flank can do. The adversary is devising new ways to ask: 'Did God really say that?' and 'Would God really hold this from you if He loves you?' Make no mistake, the Word of Faith theology is just another Eden-like assault on God's Word.

Similarly, the prosperity gospel is an attack on truth from the flank. Those preaching this message will most likely nod in agreement with the *Chicago Statement on Inerrancy*, but then teach in ways that undercut it. Few will object to the claim that Scripture is sufficient, but their use (or abuse) of the Bible displays a lack of knowledge, a lack of confidence, or both. They're singing love ballads about Jesus to create an emotional experience and cherry-picking the Bible to find tips for moral living. They creep incrementally further from orthodoxy without seeing the danger and then fall right off the cliff.

Conservative, Reformed, evangelical, and even confessional pastors like us often look down from our high horse with an air of dismissive arrogance. We think, 'I'm sure thankful I'm not like those ignorant, blind, undiscerning sheep. My theological bearings are firm, my filters are set, and my antennae are up. I read John Piper, not *Jesus Calling*.[1]

---

1. *Jesus Calling* is a best-selling book by Sarah Young. While it contains some biblical truth and is sold by nearly all Christian retailers, Young's claim that the book contains new words from Jesus make it extremely dangerous. Tim Challies offers a full review and critique in '10 Serious Problems with

ENDURING PREACHERS IN THE BIBLE

I listen to John MacArthur, not Joyce Meyer. I pray for those misguided souls, but I'm nowhere near that ditch.'

Not so fast.

I fear the ideological underpinnings of false doctrine upon which the prosperity gospel rests are insidiously present in many of us. It lurks far beneath our sermons and is barely recognizable. Thankfully, it rarely, if ever, seeps into our public discourse or private counseling.

We aren't hoodwinked by promises of material wealth or physical health. We don't buy the lie that God can be directed and manipulated by our words. We won't baptize the promises of God's covenant with Abraham into an American context. We would never utter a phrase like, 'name-it-and-claim-it.' We're much too wise for that nonsense. But we are susceptible. I see the chink in the armor of a great number of young pastors because I once saw it in the mirror. I can summarize our inner version of prosperity teaching in one sentence: 'If I preach the faithfully, they will love the Word, love me, and the church will grow numerically.'

I appreciate the sentiment, and the sentence is not entirely false, but again, that's what makes it so dangerous. We can justify every piece of it in Scripture, but as a whole it's indefensible. Genuine believers have a Psalm 119 reaction to God's Word. They love it! A redeemed people will love their under-shepherd, warts and all. When he faithfully fulfills his ministry, they will respond with a Hebrews 13:17 attitude. The faithful preaching of the Word

---

Jesus Calling,' accessed on 10-23-18. https://www.challies.com/articles/10-serious-problems-with-jesus-calling/

will yield a harvest. They may come by the thousands like the crowd in Jerusalem in Acts 2 or one-by-one like Saul of Tarsus in Acts 9, but if we preach, God will save.

Here's how it plays in the mind of a young pastor.

If I preach expository sermons, my new church will love it. It may take a few months to adjust, but by the end of the first year they'll be on the edge of their seats begging for more. That is, unless they're God-hating false believers. If I preach expository sermons, my new church will love me. They'll bear with me as I improve, appreciate my eccentricities, respect my biblical fidelity, and view me the way [insert well-known pastor's church] appreciates [insert well-known pastor's name]. That is, unless they're heartless unregenerate church 'members' who wouldn't even appreciate [insert same well-known pastor's name]. If I preach expository sermons, we'll need to start a building campaign to accommodate the crowds. The church has already been planted, I'll water the seeds, and God will give the increase. We better get ready for some 1 Corinthians 3:6-7 around here. That is, unless these fields are irrecoverably dry and hardened by sin.

Sure, I will face a few detractors along the way. Some folks will try to hold us back and beat me down. But the two-edged sword will cut hearts like it did in Acts 2 and droves of people will regularly cry out, 'What must I do to be saved?' Once the pulpit ministry is recalibrated, the true sheep will flock (yep, that's a pun) to the faithful preaching of the word. Indeed, 'God will build his church and the gates of hell will not prevail against it' (Matt 16:18). We'll have a repeat of Nehemiah 8-10. I'll read and explain the Word, the people will eagerly receive it (maybe even stand for half-a-day to hear it), and the response of repentance

and obedience will be undeniable. Biblical exposition will
be absent no more. Revival is on the way.

Seems biblical. Except it isn't. These are independent
truths established in the biblical record, but they can't
be fixed together into a formula. It's nothing more than
a pastor's personal version of prosperity theology. 'If
I follow these steps, God will give me a desirable result.
My obedience to God will yield for me the joy of reaping
visible fruit, and plenty of it.' The optimism can almost
sound like Hebrews 11 faith, but it's not. The confidence
can sound like God-honoring hope, but it's not. The
perspective that faithful preaching will always elicit a
positive response immediately is not consistent with the
biblical record. In fact, it does little more than reflect and
feed the pastor's pride.

The temptation to fall for this false notion is especially
strong in a revitalization context. Often one of the primary
weaknesses of a declining or dying church is a lack of
biblical preaching. Thus, a pastor enters the struggling
church, diagnoses the problem, and determines to correct
the pulpit ministry. While the descent into the morass of
weak preaching likely took decades, we tend to assume the
recovery will come swiftly if we 'preach the Word.'

From the Old Testament prophets to the New Testament
apostles, the Bible is replete with examples of men who have
spoken God's Word faithfully and met resistance. This
opposition is neither accidental nor incidental as it comes by
God's sovereign hand to accomplish His plan in the world
and His purpose in the preacher. Throughout the biblical
record, God raised up human instruments to speak His

Word and to face adversity. The preaching and the struggle go hand-in-hand. Among others, God is aiming for two outcomes: proclamation of His truth and the sanctification of His preacher. His most common instruments for the former are frail, vulnerable, and struggling men and His most common instruments for the latter are apathy, hostility, and adversity. Consider a few examples.

Moses

No doubt about it, I would have hit the rock. After thirty-eight years ... pause and hear that again, thirty-eight *years*, okay, proceed ... of wandering the wilderness with the same family of complainers only to hear them whining again about water, I would have hit the rock. I'm much more tempted to make excuses for Moses for his frustrated and angry outburst than I am to judge him. I get it 100 per cent. I'm ready to boil over when my kids repeat the same patterns of disobedience for a few hours, days, or weeks. Let's rewind and recap.

Moses' ministry career was a roller coaster that displays this truth: God accomplishes His plan by raising up human instruments who will speak His Word through adversity. God calls him away from his 'secular vocation' of shepherding on the west side of the wilderness through a burning bush at the foot of Mt Sinai. Yet before the bark is cool, he's trying to convince God that it'll never work. Moses loses that debate and then receives a peaceful send-off from his father-in-law. The whole enterprise almost ends on the way back to Egypt before Zipporah saves the day with a spontaneous circumcision of their son. He and Aaron enjoy a family reunion and then team up to deliver a successful sermon before the elders of Israel. A little bumpy at the start but we're on our way up.

The first tussle with Pharaoh is an unmitigated disaster. Not only does he say no to Moses' request, he increases the hardship on the Israelite laborers. This leads the people to turn on Moses and Moses to turn on God. The wheels are coming off quickly. Apparently, he bought into the prosperity gospel long before the Crouches and the Copelands were financing tele-garbage. He had no room in his plan for failure of any kind. 'I'll preach, Pharaoh will lie down, our people will walk out, and before our herd has birthed more calves we'll be sippin' milk and eatin' honey in the land where it flows freely.' He was sorely mistaken.

God picks him up, dusts him off, and sends him back in. The next nine interactions with Pharaoh yield some waffling but no substantial change to the situation. Pharaoh and Moses are worn thin by this point and, more importantly, God is ready to act decisively. Through the tenth and final plague, God provides deliverance to His people. Egypt suffers death in every house, the Israelites are spared through the Passover lamb, and God's people exit and plunder the Egyptians on their way out the door.

Moses' roller coaster ride is just beginning. We remember the mighty deliverance at the Red Sea, but often forget the terrified cries from God's people just before it. Between the parting of the sea and reaching Mt Sinai, they traverse three more hills and valleys: bitter and then sweet water at Marah, manna and then quail to eat, and water from the rock at Massah and Meribah. In each case, the complaining people continue to struggle to trust God and His mouthpiece. The loop resumes during their time at Mt Sinai, most glaringly through the golden calf incident.

Skipping ahead thirty-eight years in the story, Numbers 20 draws together perfectly the struggle of Moses' ministry, the thread of this chapter, and the need for this book. The chapter opens with the death of Moses' sister, Miriam. From a wicker basket in the Nile to the Wilderness of Zin, these two had plenty of stories to tell. Her death is mentioned briefly, but the weight of losing a close sibling is always heavy. No time for lengthy mourning as, once again, water is in short supply and the people are quarrelling. As he had done between the Red Sea and Mt Sinai, God intended to provide water from a rock. However, in contrast to His instructions there, Moses is to 'speak' to the rock and not strike it. In anger toward the people, Moses says, 'Listen, you rebels! Must we bring water out of this rock for you?' and then hits the rock ... twice. I feel his pain, but this is no minor mistake; it exposes a lack of 'trust in [God] to demonstrate his holiness' for His people. As in Exodus 17, these waters are associated with the word 'Meribah,' which means quarrelling.

Unfortunately, the chapter isn't over. To the adversity of personal tragedy and public failure, we now add apathy and hostility from the king of Edom. He disregards Moses' summary of Israel's hardships and dismisses Moses' requests for passage through his land despite promises to stick to the main road. Finally, the chapter closes with the death of Moses' brother, Aaron, which he's told is a consequence of their recent rebellion at Meribah. As the people mourned for thirty days, I wonder how this loss landed on Israel's long-time leader.

In a short span, he buried two close siblings, dealt with the quarrelling congregation (again), and took the long road around Edom. This isn't the end of his roller coaster, but it provides a snapshot of it. Personal crises and public controversy were consistent. In Moses' ministry, God's plan to make His Word known among His people and His purpose to shape His mouthpiece through trials were inseparable.

Elijah

No doubt about it, I would have pouted under the broom tree and sulked in the cave. They hadn't had time to dispose of the burnt carcasses or sweep up confetti from the parade route and Elijah is on the run ... again. But we're getting ahead of ourselves so let's start from the beginning.

King Ahab ruled the northern kingdom for twenty-two years. He followed in and even exceeded the footsteps of those before him in doing 'evil in the sight of the Lord'. He erected an altar to Baal, constructed an Asherah, and provoked the Lord to anger. Despite his rebellion, God graciously sends His prophet Elijah to confront this evil and demonstrate His power over all other supposed gods. Elijah's ministry begins with the announcement that no rain will fall except by his command and then, by the direct command of God, he retreats to the wilderness east of the Jordan to hide out. Needless to say, Elijah's preaching is not warmly received.

After three years in hiding, during which God miraculously fed and cared for him, God commanded Elijah to return to Samaria and speak to Ahab. The ensuing showdown is legendary. Elijah challenged, mocked, defeated, and destroyed 450 prophets of Baal in one day.

God displayed His absolute power and superiority over the Canaanite gods through His prophet and brings an end to the famine. I've preached a few sermons that seemed to land well, but I've never experienced the demonstration of God's power in the form of fire from heaven and visible defeat of enemies by the sword.

Can you imagine the feelings of satisfaction and joy? His first recorded statement led to three years in hiding. Surely things will turn out differently this time. Will Ahab turn in repentance? Or will the people rise up against him and demand a righteous king?

As the rain clouds approach from the west, Ahab headed in the opposite direction for his palace at Jezreel in a chariot. Elijah, empowered by God, ran on ahead of him. Upon arrival, Ahab updated his wife Jezebel and the story turns sour. All hope of a warm and friendly reception is lost. Jezebel sent word to Elijah that she had sworn to end his life. The same man who had stood toe-to-toe with 450 prophets of Baal was afraid and ran for his life. He dropped his servant at Beersheba, walked a half-day into the wilderness, found a broom tree, and lay down to die saying, 'It is enough; now, O LORD, take away my life, for I am no better than my fathers' (1 Kings 19:4).

God isn't finished with him, though. He was awakened by an angel and fed twice, then told to keep going. After he walked forty days, he came to Mt Horeb (or as it's known, Mt Sinai). The month-long walk did not cool him down. He didn't ask to die this time, but his attitude hadn't improved much. 'Look, God, I've been an all-star prophet and it hasn't turned out well. While all Israel has abandoned you, I have maintained the right attitude and I've done what you asked.

Yet, I'm all alone. And even more, they're trying to kill me! This is not exactly what I had in mind.' Can I get an 'Amen,' weary pastor?

God responds to Elijah with a gracious, quiet word and another assignment. 'Get up and go back to work for I have thousands of men and women that you know nothing about.' This narrative isn't the sum total of Elijah's ministry, but it's enough to illustrate the point: God's plan throughout the biblical record was to make His Word known among His people and His purpose was to shape the mouthpiece through trials.

Isaiah

No doubt about it, I would have requested a different assignment. Following the confrontation of Judah's sin in the form of a pronouncement of woes, Isaiah sees a vision of the true King. The transcendent God is surrounded by angels who are always declaring His worth and ever ready to serve Him. Struck by his unworthiness, Isaiah cries out in humble acknowledgement of sin and receives God's gracious forgiveness. Then, clearly and dramatically, God asks for a servant. Isaiah is ready to go. 'Over here, Lord. I got you. I'll go!' (in 6:8).

Often the study of this passage ends with Isaiah's surrender, but the final four verses of the chapter are critical for our purpose. God gives him the assignment: preach to a stubborn people and through your ministry the situation will worsen. No positive results, Isaiah, only dull hearts, deaf ears, and blind eyes.

For the first year, right? I mean, I know how dull they are. I just pointed out their apostasy and the bitter fruit it has produced. But I'll get rolling with some 'Thus says the Lord ...' and they'll fall in repentance for sure. Not because I'm a great preacher, but God, your Word will accomplish what you purpose for it. So, how long are we talking about dull, deaf, and blind? Until the whole place lies in ruins.

We don't know for sure how long Isaiah's ministry would last. It began around the time of Uzziah's death in 740 B.C. and stretched through the Assyrian invasion in 701. Per Jewish tradition, he died during persecution under Manasseh sometime after 687 and based on the mention of Sennacherib's death (in 37:38), it's possible he lived past 681. He saw the fall of Israel to the north, faced the Assyrian threat in Judah, and learned of the Babylonian exile 100 years before it came to pass. He enjoyed a few mountain peaks along the way, including the revival under Hezekiah, but the vast majority of his ministry – between forty and sixty years – was steady decline and impending doom. How long, O Lord? He ministered for decades in a field that I don't think I would've lasted six months.

The list goes on and on, but I think we get the point. God used the mouths of men to make known His Word and used adversity to mold the men. The New Testament brings more of the same.

The Twelve

No doubt about it, I would've second-guessed my vocational decision. I try to imagine witnessing the extraordinary and miraculous catch of fish out of the Sea of Galilee and then hearing, 'Drop your nets and let's go fish for men.' While it may appear risky and impulsive, it was a reasonable decision based on all the available facts at the time. I'm pretty sure He is *the* Messiah, so if He wants me on His team, I'm game for whatever He asks.

The early days of Jesus' public ministry seem more like a carnival than a church service. Throngs of people flocked to Him everywhere He went. What was not to love? He walked from place-to-place healing diseases, casting out demons, and preaching fantastic messages based on the Hebrew Scriptures. He was kind, compassionate, and warm. He stooped to help the outcast, spoke in ways the average person could understand, and conversed with the brightest theological minds. And the twelve had a front-row seat. They were one-part spectator, one-part servant, one-part student, and eventually, one-part sent-one. Who, in their right mind, would turn down that invitation?

The euphoria didn't last, though. For the most part, the admiration of the crowd remained, but their enthusiasm began to wane. They still loved Jesus' miracles and healings, but His messages didn't always resonate and sometimes they even drove people away. Some of His stories were confusing and even confounding on purpose. Still more, a few messages were downright confrontational. If He'd just find a third way, a moderating position.

After the twelve learned through instruction and observation, Jesus sent them out on their own ministry assignment. Essentially, do what you've seen me do: preach, heal, raise, cleanse, and cast out. Some will welcome you and others won't, but don't worry about the response. Peter probably had one foot on the path ready to get started. I can almost hear him saying, 'Got it, let's roll ... Oh, there's more?' Jesus' words of instruction in Matthew 10:16-25 dropped like a lead balloon.

The opening word picture was graphic and attention-grabbing: 'I am sending you out as sheep in the midst of wolves.' Yikes. 'They will hate you, mistreat you, and seek to kill you. Don't fear and don't stop preaching because it's all part of the plan.' Again, I would have been second-guessing my decision back on the beach. Do you have any other job openings?

Their first ministry circuit did not produce this type of intense opposition, but the decades to follow would prove the prophetic nature of these words. In the interest of space, I'll skip the point-by-point detail of the apathy and hostility they faced. But between the record in Acts and the testimony of the church fathers, it's clear that the apostles join the Old Testament prophets in demonstrating that God makes His Word known through human preachers and exposes these preachers to great adversity. Once again, these are twin truths.

Paul

No doubt about it, Paul's ministry makes even the toughest field in our culture look like a day at the park. Perhaps you're reading this book and looking for a life-line to grab because you feel like the ship is halfway under the water already. You know perseverance is required, but you wonder if you can actually finish the race. Consider Paul.

We know almost nothing about his first years of training and ministry in Arabia and Damascus, but two facts emerge from Acts 9: he began proclaiming Jesus immediately and he escaped through a hole in the wall because of hostile opposition. We skip ahead several years to his first missionary journey to find some Jews shrugging off his synagogue sermons and others hurling stones at his head. Upon returning to his home base in Antioch, he's confronted with internal conflict in the church. Unfortunately, the controversy wasn't limited to one place but was swirling throughout the churches, including the fledgling congregations he just planted. Before traveling to Jerusalem for the council meeting, he fired off a passionate letter to address the false teaching that infiltrated the Galatian churches leading them to abandon the gospel he preached and to defend himself against the accusations against him and his ministry.

The meeting in Jerusalem produces a good result, but before he gets back out on the missionary trail he endures a sharp disagreement with his closest ministry partner that ends in separation. The two subsequent missionary journeys yield more of the same: bold proclamation, personal adversity, and violent hostility. Near the close of his third journey, he summarizes his struggles in two passages in a letter to the church in Corinth.

> We are afflicted in every way, but not crushed; perplexed, but not driven to despair; persecuted, but not forsaken; struck down, but not destroyed.... Are they servants of Christ? I am a better one – I am talking like a madman – with far greater labors, far more imprisonments, with countless beatings, and often near death. Five times I received at the hands of the Jews the forty lashes less one. Three times I was beaten with rods. Once I was stoned. Three times I was shipwrecked; a night and a day I was adrift at sea; on frequent journeys, in danger from rivers, danger from robbers, danger from my own people, danger from Gentiles, danger in the city, danger

in the wilderness, danger at sea, danger from false brothers; in toil and hardship, through many a sleepless night, in hunger and thirst, often without food, in cold and exposure. And, apart from other things, there is the daily pressure on me of my anxiety for all the churches (2 Cor. 4:8-9; 11:23-28).

These are staggering paragraphs, especially when we consider that he wrote them before his arrest in Jerusalem, before his imprisonment in Caesarea, before his shipwreck on the island of Malta, before his Roman imprisonment, and well before he wrote the letters to Timothy. In one of the final paragraphs we have from Paul (2 Tim. 4:9-18), he writes of recent physical suffering, desertion of close ministry partners, fierce opposition from within the church, and incredible loneliness. Adversity in the form of apathy and hostility weren't exceptions during his thirty-plus years in ministry, they were the rule.

In our survey of the biblical record, Paul stands as the final, and perhaps the clearest, example of the truth: God plants His preachers in difficult fields to proclaim His Word and purify the preacher. In one sense, all preachers stand in this line. It's part of God's purpose to shape us and to use us to shape others. In another sense, those who give their lives to the ministry of church revitalization can commiserate more clearly with this list of biblical saints. The struggle may not be greater, but it often feels lonelier. The pain may not be more intense, but it can feel more severe under the cloud of failure that we often feel. Pastors, take heart when you face snarls and scowls because you're not alone.

2

ENDURING PREACHERS IN CHURCH HISTORY

We tend to think that the preachers from history who are remembered fondly today were equally beloved by their churches. Even a cursory review of church history exposes the folly of that perspective. In fact, we often know of these men because they remained faithful despite great difficulty. Suffering comes with the territory, but faithfulness is not guaranteed. One of God's instruments for helping us persevere in the present is the cloud of enduring witnesses in the past. Before we turn to three pictures of pastoral faithfulness, let Martin Luther's description of this difficulty give us context:

> How difficult an occupation preaching is. Indeed, to preach the Word of God is nothing less than to bring upon oneself all the furies of hell and of Satan, and therefore also of .... every power of the world. It is the most dangerous kind of life to throw oneself in the way of Satan's many teeth.[1]

---

1. Martin Luther as quoted by David Prince 'Lead from the Front: The Priority of Expository Preaching' in *A Guide to Church Revitalization,* edited by R. Albert Mohler, Jr., (Louisville, KY: SBTS Press; 2015), 32-33.

Enduring Hostility: Charles Simeon

Only God knows of the countless men who have labored in difficult fields over the centuries, but few recorded stories match the hostility Charles Simeon endured at the hands of his own congregation. Their relationship began poorly and only descended from there. Despite vocal opposition from the church, the bishop appointed Simeon as Minister of Holy Trinity Church in Cambridge in November 1782. In the months leading to this appointment, the parishioners not only opposed him, they petitioned the bishop to have their Curate, John Hammond, installed as minister. Hammond had served them in this role as an assistant for some time and they made their preference for him clearly known.

When the petition was denied, they turned to political maneuvering in an attempt to manipulate the bishop. At that time, the primary income source for a minister came from the lectureship in the church. While the Lecturer was almost always the minister, the congregation held the authority to select that person separate from the bishop's appointment. Knowing of the bishop's intent to appoint Simeon, the congregation threatened to give the lectureship, and thus the primary source of income, to Hammond no matter who was appointed as their minister.

Aware of the brewing controversy, Simeon expressed his desire for peace and willingness to step aside to the congregation. He even considered writing to the bishop to this end. Ultimately, he decided to await the bishop's response to the church's petition and accept his decision. The bishop was undeterred by the church's threat and offered the position to Simeon. In addition, he made clear to Simeon that regardless of whether he accepted the post, Hammond would not receive it.

All parties followed-through on their promises. Bishop Yorke appointed Simeon. Simeon accepted the position. The congregation appointed Hammond as Lecturer. Hammond taught every Sunday afternoon and received income from it. Derek Prime captures the setting well. 'Scarcely a worse start to a ministry could be imagined. The sense of hostility was tangible. His pastoral wish to visit people was impossible because of their bitterness at his appointment: none would admit him to their homes.'[2]

The intensity of the hostility was matched only by its longevity. Biographer Handley Moule remarks, 'Long and painful was the siege laid against Simeon's activity and influence.'[3] He assumed his responsibility to preach on Sunday mornings, but the parishioners stood in his way. They refused to attend and even locked their pews so no one could use their seats. Simeon responded by bringing in benches and seats at his own expense only to have them thrown out by the churchwardens. After several months, he began Sunday evening lectures from the Scripture, but again the churchwardens tried to prevent him. They shut the doors on him and on one occasion they even locked them and left with the key. This opposition lasted more than a decade. Hammond continued as Lecturer for five years and the job was then given to a parishioner's son

---

2. Derek Prime, *Charles Simeon: An Ordinary Pastor of Extraordinary Influence.* (Leominster: Day One, 2011), 46.

3. Handley Moule, *Charles Simeon: Pastor of a Generation* (Fearn, Ross-shire: Christian Focus, 1997), 42.

instead of Simeon. He would not assume that responsibility until 1794, twelve years after his appointment as minister.

What was Simeon's response to this open hostility? He did not strike back. He patiently, persistently preached. After coming to check on him, his mentor, Henry Venn, wrote, 'He preaches twice a week ... and his people are indeed of an excellent spirit – merciful, loving, and righteous.'[4] He ascended the pulpit every Sunday morning to exposit God's Word. And in an extremely rare move, he held a Sunday evening lecture in a large room in another church's parish. Even more, Simeon committed himself to the Lord trusting in Him without angst or bitterness. For more than fifty years, Simeon faithfully preached and taught the Bible. The essence of his ministry shines through his twenty-one-volume work, *Horae Homileticae*, that contains chapter-by-chapter commentary and sermon outlines on every book of the Bible.

Simeon's words are as remarkable as they are powerful:

> I wished rather to suffer than to act; because in suffering I could not fail to be right; but in acting I might easily do amiss. Besides, if I suffered with a becoming spirit, my enemies, though unwittingly, must of necessity do me good; whereas if in acting I should have my own spirit unduly exercised, I must of necessity be injured in my own soul, however righteous my cause might be.[5]

> Certain it is, that the saints whom God has most approved, have been most abundantly exercised in different manners for the trial of their faith: and they

---

4. Prime, 47.

5. Moule, 36.

who are most earnest in prayer for grace, are most often afflicted, because the graces which they pray for, e.g. faith, hope, patience, humility, etc., are only to be wrought in us by means of those trials which call forth several graces into act and exercise; and in the very exercise of them they are all strengthened and confirmed.[6]

[God] knew the real desire of my heart; he knew that I only wished to fulfil his will. I told him a thousand times over that I did not deprecate persecution; for I considered that as the necessary lot of all who would 'live godly in Christ Jesus'; and more especially, of all who would preach Christ with fidelity;[7]

Pastors, let Simeon's example and testimony spur us on. Even in the face of a hostile congregation, do not grow weary in doing good, for in due season God will reap His harvest.

Enduring Apathy: Jonathan Edwards

On July 8, 1741, Edwards delivered one of the most famous sermons in history at Enfield, Connecticut. Despite the winds of revival sweeping through New England and all around, this town remained virtually untouched. A group of ministers responded to the town's reputation of resistance to the extraordinary work of God. One account alleged that Edwards was not originally scheduled to preach, but as providence would have it, preach he did. This sermon was a spark that ignited the flames of revival in that town even while he preached.

---

6. Prime, 48.

7. Ibid., 47.

The townspeople who filed into the church building were described by one eyewitness as 'thoughtless and vain,' failing to treat one another with even 'common decency.'[8] The meeting lacked the notes of readiness, attentiveness, and seriousness that were prevalent during the First Great Awakening. Then Edwards began. He spoke of mankind's awful plight as rebels against God, deserving the fires of hell every moment. Edwards warned them, 'God is under no manner of obligation to keep [a person] a moment from eternal destruction.' He continued:

> That world of misery, that lake of burning brimstone is extended abroad under you. There is the dreadful pit of the glowing flames of the wrath of God; there is hell's wide gaping mouth open; and you have nothing to stand upon, nor anything to take hold of: there is nothing between you and hell but the air; 'tis only the power and mere pleasure of God that holds you up.[9]

Through the vivid imagery and clear presentation, God awoke the people to the reality of their situation and to His wonderful grace in Christ. Even while Edwards preached, the weeping was so loud that he stopped preaching while other ministers moved among the crowd praying with individuals and leading them to profess saving faith in Christ.[10]

---

8. George M. Marsden, *Jonathan Edwards: A Life* (New Haven & London, Yale University Press, 2003), 220.

9. Jonathan Edwards, 'Sinners in the Hands of an Angry God.' Monergism.com, accessed on 10-25-18 https://www.monergism.com/thethreshold/sdg/pdf/edwards_angry.pdf

10. Josh Moody, 'This Day in History: Jonathan Edwards Preaches 'Sinners in

This sermon has become one of the most famous in the history of the church, but most don't know that Edwards delivered the same sermon to his congregation at Northampton a few weeks prior. His church, already enjoying the movement of revival, responded quite differently to the message. There was no crying, no weeping, no dramatic response, no memorable effects; only the normal reception of the faithful exposition of the Word. In their defense, some have noted that in preaching to his congregation, the delivery and application were markedly different. The fiery appeals of Enfield were replaced with pastoral encouragement to continue in repentance and faith. While not glossing over the differences, it is a telling example of the way this congregation under-appreciated the gift that Edwards was to them.

The anecdote prepares us for the story of the end of Edwards' ministry in Northampton. Many know Edwards only for his famous sermon, but scholars and historians routinely call him America's finest theologian and among the most brilliant minds ever born in North America. Despite his exceptional gifts, his church voted to remove him after more than twenty years of leading them as pastor. The context of his removal was complex, but the congregation's apathy toward his preaching is evident as we look back on the situation.

He served as an apprentice for two years under his well-known and widely respected grandfather, Solomon Stoddard. After his death in 1729, Edwards began to lead

---

the Hands of an Angry God." Crossway, July 8, 2018. Accessed on 10-25-18 https://www.crossway.org/articles/this-day-in-history-jonathan-edwards-preaches-sinners-in-the-hands-of-an-angry-god/.

the congregation in his mid-twenties. Over the next decade, God did a surprising work in that church. From December 1734 through the middle of 1735, they saw hundreds of conversions through the unmistakable movement of the Spirit.[11] The fruit of revival was evident through his ministry and they enjoyed remarkable seasons of extraordinary blessing for more than a decade.

The clouds of controversy eventually rose. In studying the Scripture over the years, Edwards became convinced that the Lord's Supper was only for genuine believers. The church would never adopt the shift away from open communion, which they practiced under Stoddard's leadership. After a couple of years of conflict, the ministerial council dismissed him in the summer of 1750 after discovering that only 10 per cent of the parish wanted him to remain.[12] Access to the Lord's table was the central issue, but Marsden notes that 'there were pent-up resentments that came pouring out when the occasion arose.'[13] Many long-time members and friends of Stoddard thought of Edwards as an arrogant successor who sullied his grandfather's legacy. Edwards admitted that his mistakes and failures stirred the controversy, but it was not enough to stem the tide of angst against him.

And so, after two decades and a bitter end to his pastorate at Northampton, he preached a 'Farewell Sermon' from 2 Corinthians 1:14 that John Piper lauded as 'one of the

---

11. Peter Beck, 'Jonathan Edwards (1703-58): Faithful to the End,' in *12 Faithful Men*, edited by Collin Hansen and Jeff Robinson (Grand Rapids: Baker, 2018), 63-64.

12. Ibid., 69.

13. Marsden, 370.

most remarkable sermons .... ever preached.'[14] Even in the emotional, final days of his ministry there, he expounded God's Word faithfully. His endurance makes it more difficult to comprehend how one of the greatest preachers and theologians in American history could be fired by his church.

His pastorate and the details of its early end were complex. To say the congregation was apathetic at every point would misrepresent what was, at times, a very fruitful and joyful ministry. But as Stephen Nichols points out, Edwards knew 'perhaps the deepest disappointment a pastor can face: to labor in love for the gospel to a congregation of yawns and sighs.'[15] In the end, the greatest pulpit ministry of the past 300 years ended abruptly and prematurely in controversy. The people were indifferent enough to his preaching to support his removal. The final years of his life were certainly not a waste. He ministered to Native Americans and wrote some of his best theological treatises. He endured the hardship of losing his pulpit in Northampton without losing his tender love for the congregation and unshakeable confidence in God.

Pastors, even in the face of an apathetic congregation, do not grow weary in doing good, for in due season God will reap his harvest.

---

14. John Piper and Justin Taylor, *A God Entranced Vision of All Things: The Legacy of Jonathan Edwards* (Wheaton: Crossway, 2004), 135.

15. Stephen J. Nichols, 'Proclaiming the Gospel and the Glory of God: The Legacy of Jonathan Edwards for Preaching,' in *For the Fame of God's Name: Essays in Honor of John Piper*, edited by Sam Storms and Justin Taylor (Wheaton: Crossway, 2010), 379.

Enduring Adversity: Charles Spurgeon[16]

If church historians made lists like sports journalists, many would argue that when it comes to preaching, outside Christ and the apostles of course, Charles Haddon Spurgeon is the GOAT. (If you're unfamiliar, it's an acronym for Greatest Of All Time.) He began preaching as a teenager and was almost immediately recognized for his extraordinary gifts, delivering more than 600 sermons before turning twenty. At the age of nineteen, he became the pastor of the largest Baptist church in London, the New Park Street Chapel. The church grew rapidly and was forced to rent venues to hold the growing crowds. Seven years into his ministry, the congregation settled into a new permanent location and became the Metropolitan Tabernacle, where he ministered for next thirty-plus years.

The reach of Spurgeon's preaching extended well beyond the five thousand people who filled this mega-church building. They translated his sermons into twenty languages and sold approximately twenty thousand copies weekly. Called the 'Prince of Preachers,' his collected sermons have been called 'the largest set of books by a single author in the history of Christianity.'[17]

Don't be misled. While the statistics make his ministry look like a breeze, it was anything but. Even outwardly fruitful ministries are not immune from the trials and

---

16. This section owes a debt to John Piper's *A Camaraderie of Confidence*. While we avoided copying from it, the influence of his work is unmistakable.

17. Eric Hayden, 'Charles Spurgeon: Did you Know?' Christianity Today. Accessed on 10-25-18. https://www.christianitytoday.com/history/issues/issue-29/charles-h-spurgeon-did-you-know.html

suffering; in fact, often the notoriety brings additional challenges. Whatever the cause, he could have, like Paul, written about affliction 'at every turn – fighting without and fear within' (2 Cor. 7:5). He faced nearly every form of adversity imaginable in one way or another.

Despite his meteoric rise and widespread popularity, he was often the subject of public criticism and ridicule. One newspaper article surmised: 'All the most solemn mysteries of our holy religion are by him rudely, roughly and impiously handled. Common sense is outraged and decency disgusted. His rantings are interspersed with coarse anecdotes.' The attacks were so prevalent that his wife was able to compile a scrapbook of them from the years 1855 and 1856.[18] Twenty years later he remarked, 'Men cannot say anything worse of me than they have said. I have been belied from head to foot, and misrepresented to the last degree.'[19]

The attacks ebbed and flowed over the years until they culminated in his withdrawal from the Baptist Union over the Downgrade Controversy in the late 1880s. He took a firm stand against associations with those who refuse to maintain doctrinal fidelity arguing that it would lead to doctrinal slippage among the orthodox. The world's most well-known preacher at the time can now be recognized as a prophet, but he could not convince his brethren. They continued down that path and even voted to censure him several months after he withdrew. Adding insult to injury, his brother seconded the Union's eventual motion to adopt a compromised doctrinal statement.

---

18. John Piper, *A Camaraderie of Confidence* (Wheaton: Crossway, 2016), 46.

19. Ibid., 47.

Despite the obvious difficulty in all these situations, the one event that seems to have caused him the most grief happened on October 19, 1856. As he stood to preach before more than ten thousand people in the Music Hall at Royal Surrey Gardens, someone in the crowd yelled, 'Fire!' In the ensuing chaos, seven people were trampled to death and dozens more injured. Many blamed him. The burden so overwhelmed him that he did not preach for months and even considered quitting. Decades later, the haunting memory would return like post-traumatic stress along with feelings of responsibility and guilt.[20]

Adverse life circumstances at home created burdens for Spurgeon as well. His wife Susannah gave birth to their twin boys in 1856, but they were not able to have more. Her health declined significantly in her mid-thirties to the point that she was rarely able to hear him during the last twenty-five years of his ministry.

The fighting without was matched by physical adversity within, in the form of gout, rheumatism, and Bright's disease. The onset of gout came in his mid-thirties and grew worse over the years causing him to vacate his pulpit for months at a time to recover. When he died at only fifty-seven, he was in France attempting to recuperate from the ongoing maladies in his diseased and failing body.[21] This man with a sharp mind and booming voice was no superman and reminders of his frailty were constant throughout his ministry in London.

---

20. Zach Eswine, 'Charles Spurgeon (1834-92): Faithful in Sorrow', in *12 Faithful Men*, edited by Collin Hansen and Jeff Robinson (Grand Rapids: Baker, 2018), 131.

21. Piper, 46.

His inward adversity was not isolated to physiological matters; however, Spurgeon also wrestled with 'spiritual sorrows.' As pastor of the same church for thirty-eight years, he knew well the minor disappointments of shepherding unfaithful members and leading a large congregation. His 'mental miseries' were much worse, though. The dark clouds of depression covered him first at the ripe age of twenty-four when he described his spirit as 'sunken so low that I could weep by the hour like a child, and yet I knew not what I wept for.'[22] This battle raged throughout his life making him feel at times that God had deserted him and at others that God was smiting him.[23]

Despite all this adversity, Spurgeon endured to the end as pastor of Metropolitan Tabernacle. A casual glance at his vitae might lead to the assumption that he sailed through life untouched by the ordinary trials of ministry. But any such thoughts are sorely misguided. Pastors, even in the face of a mountain of adversity, do not grow weary in doing good, for in due season God will reap His harvest.

Do Not Grow Weary

The list goes on and on. John Calvin's ministry in Geneva, which began because of Farel's famous, ominous, and over-reaching threat, was interrupted for more than three years when he was dismissed by the congregation and continued through more than a decade of resistance upon his hesitant return. If you think Calvin's name is controversial today,

---

22. Piper, 48.

23. Eswine, 129.

you should've been in Geneva in the middle years of the sixteenth century. Yet, he endured.

George Whitefield's thundering and effective preaching ministry faced opposition in the form of dead cats thrown at him while preaching and slanderous attacks from church leaders. He was present to hear one bishop in London speak 'all manner of evil' against him falsely drawing parallels with a host of deviant groups including one that was 'guilty of the most notorious incest and murder.'[24] Yet, he endured.

As we well know, hostility, apathy, and adversity are not problems that remain in the past. Every well-known expositor in the last 100 years has faced his share of all three. John MacArthur faced an attempted coup by a group of young pastors he was training and a call for his resignation by an elder a few years later.[25] John Piper suffered with cancer and 'species of pride.'[26] Tom Carson, the relatively unknown father of New Testament scholar D. A. Carson, labored in obscurity.[27] Yet, these men endured.

These men are only a few from the diverse myriad of preachers and pastors throughout church history who have preached the Word of God and faced opposition for it. They are not exactly like one another and none are

---

24. L. Tyerman, *The Life of Rev. George Whitefield*, (New York: Anson D. F. Randolph & Company, 1877), 397-98.

25. John MacArthur, Criticism: 'A Pastor's All-too-Common Companion,' Delivered at Together for the Gospel, April 2018. Accessed 10-25-18, http://t4g.org/media/2018/04/criticism-pastors-common-companion/.

26. John Piper, 'John Piper's Upcoming Leave.' Desiring God, accessed 10-25-18 https://www.desiringgod.org/articles/john-pipers-upcoming-leave

27. D. A. Carson, *Memoirs of an Ordinary Pastor* (Wheaton: Crossway, 2008).

exactly like you or me. Our goal is not for you to identify with or emulate one of them, but to see a thread of truth. Some preachers will be well-known, while others more obscure. Some will preach classic expositional sermons, while others more textual exposition. Some will have extraordinary gifts, while others more ordinary gifts. But we are bound together by a commitment to proclaim God's truth and the need to endure.

Brother pastor, you're not alone.[28] Your struggle is neither unique nor a surprise. Albert Mohler insightfully summarizes the danger and difficulty of our calling to preach faithfully.

> This line of work has a nasty way of getting you into trouble. It seems that the more faithful one is in preaching, the more trouble one encounters. Why? There is conflict and controversy. You preach the Word. You did not come up with it. This is not your opinion, and it is not something you came up with in order to offend people. You are simply preaching the Word. After all, that is your assignment. So you preach the truth, and the next thing you know you are on the front page of the papers. You are the subject of gossip for the deacons and their wives; even the youth group is up in arms over whatever you said. Conflict and controversy are always hard, and they again tend to be correlated to faithfulness in preaching.

---

28. For more reading in this vein, we commend two resources we have quoted from in these pages. A compilation of John Piper's seven books in the 'The Swans are Not Silent' series was released by Crossway in 2018 under the title, *21 Servants of Sovereign Joy.* Hansen and Robinson's work *12 Faithful Men* is also excellent. In fact, it was a timely resource to aid in our writing *Facing Snarls and Scowls.*

The harder you work at it, the greater the risk, the higher the stakes.[29]

'Let us not grow weary of doing good, for in due season we will reap, if we do not give up' (Gal. 6:9).

---

29. R. Albert Mohler, Jr., 'The Primacy of Preaching' in *Feed my Sheep* (Orlando: Soli Deo Gloria Publications, 2002), 10.

PART 2

DO NOT GIVE THEM A GOOD REASON TO HATE YOUR PREACHING

3

Bad Preaching Deserves Rebuke

Snarls and scowls are never the appropriate response from the people of God to the preaching of His Word. We ought to drink in sermons like a soaking, summer rain. This is not to say that we should blindly and naïvely receive them. We ought also to listen discerningly and recognize sermons that are lacking. In these cases, we are called to critique, confront, and even rebuke bad sermons with gentleness and love with the goal of building up the preacher and ultimately edifying the church. Preachers and congregations benefit from this type of accountability and training from godly saints sitting under the care of imperfect under-shepherds.

I (James) will never forget one such encounter in my ministry. I had preached the first of two services on a Sunday morning from a narrative passage of Scripture. I don't recall the exact text, but I remember the conversation with a godly lady immediately afterward. As was my practice at the time, I preached the passage by working through the story, summarizing smaller sections, and then reading all or part of the Scripture that supported it. After the final song concluded, I was greeting folks as the room was emptying and refilling in preparation for round two. With Christlike grace, humility, and tenderness, a lady I knew well asked if she could share her thoughts on my sermon. I could tell she was nervous and a little uncomfortable in approaching, but that she felt compelled to do so.

Before I share her thoughts, please know that my preaching ministry had not been well received up to that point. I'll share more of my story in Chapter 7, but suffice it to say, I'd seen snarls and scowls, heard plenty of criticism, and was growing calloused to it. I expected some version of what I'd heard before and I was not really in the mood to receive it. I knew better than to shrug her off rudely, but I'm ashamed that I mentally dismissed her. I thought some version of: 'I have a doctorate in preaching, ma'am. Either your comment will be what I already know or something I don't need to hear. While you join the chorus of *snarlers* and *scowlers*, I'll stand here, nod politely, and try to keep a straight face while I formulate a gracious verbal response.'

The conversation did not go as I had planned; instead, God used her comment to shape the way I preach and to sanctify my heart. To paraphrase her constructive criticism: 'When you preach, read the Scripture before you tell us about it. That way it is primary and your comments are secondary. I appreciate what you have to say, and it's helpful, but show me what the Bible says first.' She was absolutely right and wonderfully gracious to say it. She wasn't snarling or scowling; she was loving. While I'd argue that my approach fit under the definition of expository preaching, one aspect of my delivery was 'bad.'

This anecdote demonstrates that it's possible for pastors with sound theology, good training, and a genuine desire to honor God to preach bad sermons. Sometimes we'll need to overhaul the entire message and at other times only smaller adjustments are warranted. Our homiletical theory can be wonky, our sermon preparation lacking, our content insufficient, or our delivery ineffective. Nevertheless, standing in front of the congregation and talking about biblical ideas with pure motives each week is not necessarily fulfilling our ministry faithfully. The hostility, apathy, and adversity will often come from ungodly people bristling under the truth of God's Word and we want to prepare you to persevere in these difficult fields. But before you dismiss every negative reaction to your preaching as a snarl or a scowl, always consider that it could be a reaction – although inappropriate in its delivery – to *bad* preaching.

Since preaching is a vital instrument for God's work in individuals and His church, the last thing needed in the church, and particularly in revitalization settings, is the unhealthy concoction of bad preaching and snarling congregants. Thus, let's eliminate the one under our control.

The Necessity of Preaching

Preaching is part of every pastor's job description. Some have the joy of delivering sermons every week while others preach less frequently. But biblically-speaking, to be a pastor is to be a preacher. The pulpit ministry has always been at the heart of the pastor's ministry. Paul encourages Timothy to 'devote himself to the public reading of Scripture, to exhortation, to teaching' (1 Tim. 4:13) and to 'preach the word; be ready in season and out of season; reprove rebuke, and exhort, with complete patience and teaching' (2 Tim. 4:2).

Preaching, therefore, is not merely on the pastor's list of responsibilities; it is always at the top. Most churches acknowledge this fact, but I doubt whether many realize how critical preaching is for the church's health and vitality. Al Mohler speaks definitively when he contends that 'This is not to say that .... there are not even other priorities; but there is one central, non-negotiable, immovable, essential priority, and that is the preaching of the Word of God.'[1]

Preaching is primary for the pastor because of its place in Christianity. As John Stott has famously written, 'preaching is indispensable to Christianity.' A local church will not survive without the consistent explanation and application of the Scripture. It may take a few generations to die out completely, but a church's long-term viability is irrevocably tied to faithfulness in the pulpit. Jesus presents this truth through a vivid picture of contrast between the wise and foolish builders in Matthew 7. The man (or church) who builds on the foundation of God's words will enjoy a firm base. The man (or church) who ignores His words will collapse on the shifting sand under the weight of trials and difficulty.

Preaching is also indispensable because of its place in the church's ordinary ministry. The proclamation of the Word undergirds every other aspect of pastoral ministry. Sunday morning isn't enough to make disciples adequately, but without God-honoring pulpit ministry every other

---

1. Mohler, 16.

endeavor will suffer. The ministry of the Word forms the centerpiece in the regular congregational gathering, which is the hub of the church's ministry wheel. Service ministries, Bible study groups, individual discipleship, and age-graded ministries project outward like spokes extending and applying the expository ministry. Barring an extraordinary work of God, the preaching ministry will serve to limit or catapult these other ministries. Preaching is never an incidental aspect of church's ministry; instead, it is a rudder that steers the ship.

To this end, Mark Dever argues in *Nine Marks of a Healthy Church* that expositional preaching 'is far and away the most important' of all the marks 'because if you get this one right, all of the others should follow.' He continues, 'This is so important that if you were to miss this one and happen to get the other eight marks right, in a sense they would be accidents.'[2] Preaching forms the central spring flowing from the well of biblical truth that waters and nourishes the local church.

Finally, preaching is primary because of its place in the extraordinary work of God among His people. Every great move of God in the Bible and church history was stimulated or carried along by faithful preaching. In addition to serving as a steady, ordinary means of grace for the church, preaching is a catalyst for God's work of renewal. As D. Martyn Lloyd-Jones shows in the opening chapter of his classic work, 'a revival of true preaching has always heralded

---

2. Mark Dever, *Nine Marks of a Healthy Church*, 3rd Edition. (Wheaton, Crossway, 2013), 42-43.

these great movements in the history of the Church.[3] From the base of Mount Sinai to the people of Nehemiah's day to the explosion of the church recorded in Acts to the recovery of theological fidelity in the Reformation to the expansion of the church during The Great Awakening, the preaching of the Word was always central to God's extraordinary work.

Indeed, the Spirit is like the wind in that He moves in ways we cannot see, comprehend fully, or foresee, as Jesus explained in the conversation with Nicodemus (John 3:8). But while we cannot manipulate God with formulas, the history of His work among His people reveals that preaching and prayer are essential elements to the outpouring of His special grace. The dates, circumstances, and details of revival vary, but faithful exposition of God's Word is a common thread. Which brings us to the thrust of this chapter; namely, the need for *good* preaching.

Practically and biblically, then, preaching is necessary. But again, it's not enough to stand in front of the congregation for twenty to thirty (or even forty to fifty) minutes each week and talk about spiritual matters. As pastors, our calling is to proclaim the Word of God faithfully. Simply put, we must labor to develop and deliver good sermons.

What is Good Preaching?

I'm finishing this chapter as I ward-off an afternoon lull from eating a combo platter of brisket, pulled pork, and ribs. After years of hearing friends brag about the superiority of it, I finally made it to downtown Dallas to

---

3. Lloyd-Jones, *Preaching and Preachers* (Grand Rapids: Zondervan, 1972), 24-25.

experience Texas-style smoked meat. I'm not ready to hand over any kind of award, but it certainly did not disappoint. It's tough for me to select a favorite, though, because as a barbeque enthusiast I appreciate nearly all varieties. When it comes to grading it, I look at two primary combinations: tenderness and taste of the meat and heat and sweet in the sauce. *Good* barbeque falls apart easily and has a deep smoky flavor complemented by a sauce that is mostly sweet with a kick of spice. I can handle mustard-based, tangier sauces, but sweet is definitely preferred.

Perhaps I think too deeply about my food, but I raise barbeque because it's on my mind (or in my stomach) and because it illustrates the inherent subjectivity of the word *good*. This description may seem like an impossible target because it moves based on the evaluator. Instincts tell us that the quality of a sermon, like the quality of brisket or pork, is in the eye of the beholder. What's good to me may not be good to you. To be sure, if you ask a congregation to define or describe a *good* sermon, you'll receive a wide variety of responses grounded in different facets of sermon development, design, and delivery. It might seem odd, but we've chosen a seemingly subjective term – *good* – on purpose because unlike barbeque, there is an objective source for determining sermon quality. Our concern is not to aim for what the average church-goer (in Kentucky or Texas or anywhere) wants or even what would be appreciated by the largest number of people. Instead, we measure the quality of a sermon by the degree to which it fulfills the biblical ideal.

But even then, the biblical standard for preaching is not presented straightforwardly in a single text. Rather, we're forced to piece it together using a host of examples and a few direct exhortations. While certainly not exhaustive, we hang our thoughts here on five characteristics of preaching gleaned from Scripture.

First and primarily, *good* preaching is expository preaching. We wholeheartedly affirm Stott's declaration that 'all true Christian preaching is expository preaching,' but we'll not quite go that far for the sake of argument here. Instead, we'll concede that a number of pastors are preaching sermons that convey biblical truth, point listeners to Jesus, and can be loosely described as 'Christian'. However, they do not fall under the precise definition of expository preaching.

Some sermons are built around a topic and others use a biblical text as a launching pad, then draw on other texts to craft the primary and secondary points in the sermon. So long as they teach biblical truth, these sermons can be an effective means of conveying the Christian message. Thus in one sense, they can be called 'Christian' sermons and can be powerful and effective. In fact, some settings – weddings, funerals, special meetings, etc – lend themselves to topical presentations. But again, we're not merely after sermons with Christian content, we're encouraging pastors to prepare and preach *good* Christian sermons. These types of sermons fail to reach that standard for several reasons.

These sermons may communicate truth, but they don't ground that truth clearly in the Word of God. An unmistakable link between the preacher's words and God's Word yields authority and legitimacy to the sermon in ways that are not otherwise possible. Even more, topical and textual sermons easily trend toward man-centeredness.

When the text serves the outline, in essence, the text is serving man. Finally, when the message is not clearly tethered to the text, the preacher is susceptible to passing fancies and hobby horses. He may emphasize biblical truth from time-to-time, but in the long run his preaching will be either redundant or out of balance.

These deficiencies are exacerbated over time. Comparison with physical nutrition highlights the benefits of making expository preaching a church's steady diet. A commitment to exposition forces the preacher and congregation to ingest the vegetables of difficult texts instead of the candy of our favorites. In addition, the preacher must continue learning through studying more broadly rather than returning to the same few recipes he learned in seminary. Finally, expository preaching teaches and equips the listeners to read the Scripture through modeling. As the preacher labors each week to understand and then explain the text, the congregation learns how to feed on the Word by watching his example. Once again, a preacher may speak the truth about God and even present the good news of Christ without exposing the plain meaning of a biblical text and making relevant application to his listeners. While we celebrate the announcement of God's truth, we contend that any approach not grounded in biblical exposition fails to measure up to the biblical standard for good preaching.

Second, *good* preaching glorifies God. Our aim in preaching is our aim in all areas of life: the glory of God. When the preacher directs his sermon toward any lesser end, he does a disservice to God and to the church. We don't merely preach to entertain the crowd, evangelize the lost, or edify the church. We explain and apply a biblical text to announce and enjoy the infinite value of God. In so doing, the lost are drawn to salvation and believers are built up, but those are always corollary benefits. Whether we're preaching from the Book of Judges or Paul's letter to the Romans, the ultimate goal of the sermon is the glory of God. Any sermon that aims for a lower target, even if it conveys biblical truth, is not a good sermon.

Third, *good* preaching exalts Christ. The preacher must present Christ as the only hope in any and every situation. While including thousands of stories, the Bible actually tells one long story. The individual narratives – like Noah and the big boat, Jonah and the big fish, and Jesus feeding the big crowd – fit together into one big narrative. These smaller stories are individually helpful as they convey truth about God and man. But more importantly, they provide context, curves, and content for the larger plot that is unfolding through the course of human history. The Creator God is doing something in His creation. This work is much more significant than rescuing animals two-by-two, saving a man inside a fish, or providing lunch for a hoard of people.

The larger story does not diminish the smaller ones; instead, it brings them to life in a way that makes them powerful to transform us. Many Christians in our context – twenty-first century America – have been taught Bible stories as if they are Aesop's fables. It's as if the stories of Gideon, Samson, and Esther are tales (albeit true tales) given to present morals or proverbial wisdom for living. Aesop's most famous fable is perhaps *The Hare and the Tortoise*. Who doesn't remember the slow tortoise beating the much faster hare because the former steadily plodded along while the latter slumbered in arrogance? The lingering moral of that story is certainly true, 'the race is not always to the swift.'

Despite the value of Aesop's writing for teaching and illustrating good character, it is entirely different than biblical narrative. For starters, the Bible's stories are true. Noah was an actual person who built an actual boat and survived an actual flood. Jonah was a real person who jumped into a real sea and was swallowed by a real fish. Fundamentally, the Bible is not a book of fables nor is it merely maxims for morality.

In addition, and perhaps more importantly, Aesop's fables and the Bible's stories are more profoundly different at the level of purpose. While the Bible contains wisdom for life and numerous good and bad examples to apply it, the purpose of its story-telling is much grander than making moralistic humans. The Bible is using these stories to reveal God and His grand plan to establish a Kingdom on the earth by saving sinners from His wrath. To be sure, we should acknowledge, applaud, and even emulate wise living. But a careful read of the Bible yields the distinct impression that none of the characters in the story are worth emulating. This thread of weakness and failure is not incidental; rather, it's at the very heart of each individual story and the grand story. These men and women reveal our utter hopelessness and drive us to trust in God as our only hope. The point of Bible stories is not to encourage us to be moral, but to reveal our immorality and lead us to trust in God. The stories point beyond a simplistic moral to the divine Savior.

This grand narrative culminates in one Person who is the perfect example of wise living fulfilling God's standard in every way. Of course, this One is Jesus. But even He is not shown primarily as a model to follow; instead, He is presented as altogether different than every other person in the narrative. The stories about Him in the Gospels don't call us to be like Him as much as they demonstrate how unlike Him we really are. While there is a call to follow Him and pattern our lives after His, that call is grounded in the unique work He did by dying for our sin and rising from the dead. He becomes a model for us only after we acknowledge our hopelessness, embrace Him by faith, and receive the Holy Spirit. Then, and only then, do we have the ability or power to follow His example.

The pastor mustn't simply take the Bible, re-tell one of the great stories, and find principles for living. He must preach the stories as windows that reveal God, mirrors that reflect us, and shadows that point to Jesus. He must draw listeners to a higher goal than becoming like Noah or Esther, lead them to the One who is greater than they, and call them to trust fully in Him.

Fourth, *good* preaching provides an avenue for the Holy Spirit to transform people. Preachers, particularly skilled and experienced ones, can talk for hours on end. They can engage the mind, stir emotions, and sometimes affect behavior. Even the most gifted man, however, has no capacity or capability to penetrate the heart and produce an eternal result. Despite immediate appearances, lastingly spiritual fruit is always a work of the Holy Spirit. The people may enjoy the sermon, respond with enthusiasm, and show immediate and visible signs of change, but unless the wind of the Spirit blows, any apparent results will be temporary.

So how can we make sure our sermons will be a conduit for this work? Ground them in the Word and bathe them in prayer. God's Word creates, controls, and persuades. It converts, convicts, and conforms. It is not a magic spell; it is the means God has ordained to carry out His plan and purpose. Plead with God to work in supernatural ways. Resting in the promise of Jesus in Matthew 6 that our Father will give us good things when we ask, we plead with God to feed His people with His Word. Then, in the power of God, preach the Word of God.

Fifth, *good* preaching is winsome and compelling. Even though this final characteristic might, on the surface, appear to contradict the fourth characteristic of a good sermon, it certainly does not. John Piper's most famous quote – 'God is most glorified in us when we are most satisfied in Him' – helps here. The principal characteristic of a good sermon is that it aims for God's glory. Correspondingly, God-glorifying sermons will naturally flow from men who are delighting in God as they preach them. There is no greater joy than acknowledging and announcing God's infinite worth; therefore, there is no more joyful preacher than the one who aims for God's glory in his preaching.

This joy is unmistakable, irrepressible, and infectious. Like a yawn, expressions of joy spread through a gathering of God's people as it overflows from one. No, we cannot live off another person's joy, but the visual of it in another person stirs us. We are not encouraging preachers to manufacture a stage persona or advocating for emotional manipulation. Rather, the preacher should delight in the law of the Lord in his private study and allow that joy to overflow in the pulpit. Many a seminary graduate ascends to the pulpit with the raw materials of a good sermon but fails in his preaching because he takes no joy in the God who authored the Word, the richness of the Word, or the privilege of heralding this great news. A sermon must be faithful to the text of Scripture to be good, but not all faithful sermons are actually good sermons.

Countless men have left seminary armed with the exegetical and theological tools necessary for mining the biblical text, yet they are wholly incapable of converting that rich information into a sermon that will reorient minds, redirect wills, or re-form lives. Most men will wade into the waters of pastoral ministry only to face harsh criticism of their preaching. Before dismissing the snarls and scowls as demonic opposition, re-examine your labor and consider whether you're delivering *good* sermons worthy of acceptance and celebration. Engage in serious self-evaluation to make sure you're preaching expository, God-glorifying, Christ-exalting, Holy-Spirit-empowered, and engaging sermons. In addition, entrust yourself to a few faithful brothers who will walk alongside you to improve your preaching ministry by exposing your blind-spots and challenging you to keep pressing on. You'll never perfect this craft, but faithfulness to God and love for His people should motivate us toward growth. The adversary will aim fiery darts of opposition at the preaching of God's Word, so please don't add fuel to the fire in the form of bad preaching.

4

BASICS IN EXPOSITORY PREACHING

In Chapter 3, we argued that good preaching is expository preaching and now we'll describe and define it more fully. Several excellent volumes on expository preaching have been published by capable preachers and authors, and we make no effort to supplant them. Instead, this chapter provides a primer with basic equipping to cultivate an appetite for more intense study.

We live in a moment of increasing ideological polarization. The dominant political parties in the United States move further apart with each election and seemingly on every major issue. Pew Research confirms what a casual survey of cable news reveals: 'Political polarization – the vast and growing gap between liberals and conservatives, Republicans and Democrats – is a defining feature of American politics today.'[1]

---

1. 'Political Polarization in the American Public,' Pew Research. Accessed 10-25-18.
   http://www.people-press.org/2014/06/12/political-polarization-in-the-american-public/

This polarization is also prevalent in the Christian and even evangelical subcultures with regard to a number of areas. As so-called 'progressive Christians' veer farther to the left of yesterday's theological liberals, the gap between them and conservatives grows. Among the broader spectrum of people identified as Christian, evangelicals appear increasingly strange by comparison. Even within evangelical circles, divides are growing related to a host of secondary and tertiary matters. Take preaching, for example. It seems few churches find any middle ground between topical preaching and expository preaching, holding tightly to a commitment to one or the other. While our purpose is not to sort out the positives and negatives of this situation, we draw attention to it because it introduces our aim with this chapter.

We live in an era of revival for expository preaching. More resources have been produced and a greater emphasis given to it than at perhaps any other time in church history. Haddon Robinson blazed a trail with his *magnum opus*, *Biblical Preaching*, and countless others have contributed in the last three decades. But the renewed emphasis has not led to consensus on the issue. The resistance comes from different angles for a variety of reasons. Some protest that a strict commitment to expository preaching deprives the church of topical sermons that are theologically sound and profitable. Others criticize this approach more severely. One of the most vocal and divisive critics of it has been Andy Stanley, who went so far as to call it 'cheating.'[2]

---

2. Andy Stanley, Interview with Christianity Today, accessed 8-9-18. https://www.christianitytoday.com/edstetzer/2009/march/andy-stanley-on-communication-part-2.html

Again, polarization is not helpful and that's not our intent. We concede that both approaches to preaching can have a place in the church's broader ministry; however, we remain convinced that expository preaching is the healthiest diet for regularly feeding a congregation. Therefore, as we exhort you to persevere in the pulpit, we want to be clear about the central and defining characteristics of this ministry. As we stated in the last chapter, *good* preaching is expository preaching.

Rick Warren argued almost twenty years ago that 'preaching labels' were 'meaningless' because terms like expository preaching had contradictory meanings among contemporary scholars.[3] The situation remains, and we certainly appreciate his frustration, but we don't agree with his solution. Thankfully, linguists and theologians have not jettisoned every word that has been incorrectly defined or misunderstood by a culture. To follow his advice, the term Christian should have passed away long ago amid the muck of carnal faith, works-based Catholicism, and cults like Mormonism.

Despite Warren's claim that many of the 'over thirty definitions' of expository preaching are contradictory, we can and must define this term and disallow the minority opinion to cloud the overwhelming agreement among conservative scholars.[4] While the term holds no magical value, it has and can communicate effectively if we simply ground the definition in the biblical and historical framework for preaching. So,

---

3. Michael Diduit, 'Purpose-Driven Preaching: An Interview with Rick Warren.' Preaching 17, no. 2 (2001): 14.

4. Ibid.

instead of discarding the baby of terminology with the bath water of misrepresentation, our response is to define the term appropriately and clearly. In fact, this cause is critical so that the next generation of preachers and congregants may recognize that 'expository preaching' and 'Christian preaching' are synonymous.

What is Expository Preaching?

If the term is important and confusion abounds, we must establish our baseline for understanding. Bryan Chapell provides this benchmark through one of the clearest and most thorough definitions:

> An expository sermon may be defined as a message whose structure and thought are derived from a biblical text, that covers the scope of the text, and that explains the features and context of the text in order to disclose the enduring principles for faithful thinking, living, and worship intended by the Spirit, who inspired the text.[5]

While we could easily list more than a dozen definitions that alter the wording and arrangement slightly, they all contain several non-negotiable, overlapping characteristics. Using Chapell's terms, note a few that are essential for a proper definition.

First, an expository sermon is based upon and solely dependent upon a biblical text. A preacher must build on no foundation other than God's Word. He can arrange the furniture creatively and decorate the house with pictures

---

5. Bryan Chapell, *Christ-Centered Preaching*, 2nd Edition, (Grand Rapids: Baker, 2005), 31.

that accentuate the craftsmanship of the Builder, but he has no liberty to start from any other footing. The perceived needs of the congregation, the clever illustration, a well-known cliché, and Hollywood's latest offering may make for a memorable sermon brand and entice casual attenders, but these are insufficient grounds for sculpting a sermon. The Scripture alone is worthy of being preached.

This first commitment to communicate the content of the Bible in every sermon grows from an understanding of what it is. The sixty-six books comprising the Old and New Testaments that are bound together in the Christian Bible are the breathed-out Word of the living God. These writings are not just writings; they have an authority that cannot be found anywhere else in creation. T.H.L. Parker summarizes it well in his classic work on John Calvin:

> The Scriptures are not man's guesses about the mystery of God, nor are they the conclusions that men have drawn from certain data at their disposal. On the contrary, they are the unveiling of the mystery of God by God Himself – God's gracious revelation of Himself to ignorant and sinful men.[6]

We believe the Holy Spirit inspired the human authors to write those words and that God has preserved this revelation so that we can know Him and His plan for creation. The Old Testament refers to God's Word as His creative utterance (Gen. 1:3, 6, 9, 11, 14, 20, 24, 26, 28),

---

6. T. H. L. Parker, *Portrait of Calvin.* (Minneapolis: Desiring God, 1954), 62. Accessed on 10-25-18 https://document.desiringgod.org/portrait-of-calvin-en.pdf?ts=1446647972.

as His messenger (Isa. 9:8, Jer. 1:4, Ezek. 33:7), and even as His deliverance (Ps. 107:20). God's Word is His power in action fulfilling His purpose (Isa. 55:11). The Word of God is not 'just' words on a page or information; it is God in action, personified.

Against this backdrop, John's Gospel proclaims that Jesus is the Word made flesh. He is the self-expression of God sent to make the incomprehensible God known in the world and to accomplish God's purpose. Per Jesus' testimony, He didn't come to abolish the Old Testament Scriptures, but to fulfill them. He didn't undercut their authority, significance, or value; He affirmed them as God's true and powerful Word. Following His ascension, the first believers continued to affirm the power and authority of the Hebrew Scripture while receiving new revelation for the Church. Thus, these writings – the New Testament books – carry the same weight.

These are not merely human words; they are God's Word. Unlike anything the preacher might conceive, they are 'living and active, sharper than any two-edged sword, piercing to the division of soul and of spirit, of joints and of marrow, and discerning the thoughts and intentions of the heart' (Heb. 4:12). On our best day, at our wittiest moment, with our most discerning insight, in our most passionate tone, through our most persuasive words, we cannot even approach that type of effectiveness. So please, for the sake of your congregation, don't even try. Establish every sermon on the biblical text.

Second, the sermon communicates a single concept or theme. This insight applies to all arenas of public communication because the average listener cannot follow a series of disjointed thoughts. All speeches, therefore, need a unifying idea. More than a list of random ideas or a running commentary on a given passage, the sermon must focus on a single theme and maintain unity around that theme. The well-worn illustration has been used so frequently because it works so well: it's easier to catch a baseball than a handful of sand. It's not the volume of material that makes the difference so much as the arrangement of it. Haddon Robinson helpfully clarifies, 'Sermons seldom fail because they have too many ideas; more often they fail because they deal with unrelated ideas.'[7]

But this principle applies to sermons for a more important reason: the sermon's theme comes from the original meaning of the text. Not just any old theme will do. Because of the authority of the Word, we must work to determine the author's intended meaning and build our theme on that meaning. Proper biblical interpretation, then, is necessary to our work. Here again we could write another volume explaining and describing 'proper biblical interpretation,' but that's not our purpose. Instead, we'll assume it for the sake of our argument and argue that it is an essential building block of preaching. Each sermon contains a single unifying or 'big' idea.[8]

Even more, the sermon does not merely launch from a verse or passage; the meaning of the passage *is* the message of the sermon. Or we could say, the big idea of the text is the big idea of the sermon. Whatever Paul was trying to communicate to the church through a passage in his letter

---

7. Haddon Robinson, *Biblical Preaching* (Grand Rapids: Baker, 1980), 33.

8. Ibid., 31.

becomes the central theme the preacher communicates to his congregation when he takes up that passage. Few preachers take issue with these sentences in theory, but many regularly contradict it in practice. A specific example will help.

I recently listened to a sermon by a well-known preacher of a mega-church from Galatians 6:7-8. In those verses, Paul uses a common concept in the agrarian society of the first century about reaping and sowing:

> Do not be deceived: God is not mocked, for whatever one sows, that will he also reap. For the one who sows to his own flesh will from the flesh reap corruption, but the one who sows to the Spirit will from the Spirit reap eternal life.

God embedded this truth in creation and the applications of it are virtually endless. If you sow corn, you'll reap corn. If you sow exercise, you'll reap greater health. If you sow junk food, you'll reap fat cells. If you sow materialism, you'll reap debt. If you sow distance with your spouse, you'll reap a terrible marriage. If you sow love for worldly things in your home, you'll reap kids who crave the things of the world. All of this is correct because the principle is true. But when we come to preach Galatians 6, we are not at liberty to leap to all of these places. It's improper for the preacher to hijack the illustration and make it a launching pad to preach about any topic other than Paul intended.

It's a blatant mishandling of the text to preach about weight-loss and consumer debt because Paul wasn't writing about these issues. American Christians often overeat and overspend; thus, warning them about what they will reap later is the right and loving thing to do. But that's far from Paul's point when he wrote to the churches in Galatia. He was comparing sinful, flesh-driven desires versus godly, Spirit-driven desires. He warned them that yielding to the flesh would bear the sinful fruit of 'sexual immorality, impurity, sensuality, idolatry, sorcery, enmity, strife, jealousy, fits of anger, rivalries, dissensions, divisions, envy, drunkenness, orgies, and things like these' (Gal. 5:19-21). And he exhorted them to sow, or submit to, the Spirit who brings the fruit of 'love, joy, peace, patience, kindness, goodness, faithfulness, gentleness, [and] self-control' (Gal. 5:22-23). He wasn't addressing waistlines or credit lines. The use of reaping and sowing is merely an illustration for him, but the main point is sowing the Spirit versus sowing the flesh. Therefore, when we preach that text, we must allow his illustration to illustrate his actual point, not the one we want to make. God's power to transform is in His Word, not in ours. The preacher is free to illustrate his sermon with the principle of reaping and sowing, but don't blame Paul for it. Instead, we must allow the main point of the text to be the main point of the sermon.

Third, we must go one step further. Not only is the sermon theme drawn from the theme of the text, in expository preaching the structure of the sermon also comes from the structure of the biblical text. We are bound to proclaim God's intended message and we relay it most clearly when we maintain a commitment to the manner in which He conveyed it. This deference is more than merely a stylistic attribute of our preaching; it is an act of honor for the Author.

Almost forty years ago, Eugene Lowry called for preachers to lay aside 'cherished norms about sermon anatomy' and 'form a new image of the sermon' as 'a homiletical plot, a narrative art form, a sacred story.'[9] But not every text tells a story. A survey of sermon videos from across the U.S.A. will confirm that many have listened to him. Some preachers who base their sermons on the primary point of a biblical text, look for creative ways to repackage the truth based on modern communication techniques, beliefs about learning styles, and personality preferences. Not every text is a story; therefore, not every sermon should be a story.

We are not free to allegorize the parables or use them as trampolines to land on our favorite topic. Parables are pithy stories told to drive home a point through a surprising twist. Parables are told in the context of a situation with an audience that understood the picture even if they missed the point. Preaching parables should reflect the parable's style and genre. Establish the setting. Explain the analogy. Reveal the point. Apply the truth.

The letters of the New Testament are a special gift to the Church. Intercepting Spirit-inspired correspondence from some of the brightest minds in church history to young and ordinary congregations crystalizes God's truth with power and pertinence. For us to gain most by reading other people's mail, we must understand the context of and heart behind each one. Moreover, to preach from them requires a grasp of the overall flow and specific directives that give structure and thrust to each paragraph and statement. To do

---

9. Eugene Lowry, *The Homiletical Plot: The Sermon as Narrative Art Form* (Westminster: John Knox Press, 2001), xix-xxi.

justice to any text, we must allow the logical sequence, lines of argument, and imperatives to drive the sermon. Establish the context. Expose the line of thinking. Highlight the truth. Apply the directives.

Most of the Bible is narrative. In fact, approximately 60 per cent of it is classified in that genre, which is far more than any other category.[10] When preaching these passages, Lowry's aforementioned counsel is pertinent. Let the story breathe. Blow oxygen on the flames of the narrative so that the embers roar with vivid colors and searing heat. Tell the story. Relate the author's reason for telling the story. Apply the enduring truth.

These three examples – parables, epistles, and narrative – don't exhaust the variety contained in the Bible, but they make the point. The task in expository preaching is to allow the theme, thrust, and structure of the text to provide the theme, thrust, and structure of the sermon.

Fourth, and finally, the concept that emerges from the text must be applied to both preacher and listeners. We are not giving biblical lectures or offering a running commentary. We are aiming to inform minds, instruct hearts, and influence behavior.[11] To uncover the meaning of the text would be a monumental leap forward for many modern 'preachers,' but that gain is not enough. We are not finished with our task unless and until we have brought the significance of the text home to bear on the minds, affections, and lives of the everyone present.

---

10. Julius Kim, *Preaching the Whole Counsel of God* (Grand Rapids: Zondervan, 2015), 69.

11. Ramesh Richard, *Preparing Expository Sermons* (Grand Rapids: Baker, 2001), 80.

Chapell is definitive when he writes, 'Preachers make the fundamental mistake when they assume that by providing parishioners with biblical information the people will automatically make the connection between scriptural truth and everyday lives.' And then he summarizes, 'Truth without application is useless'.[12] This aspect of preaching is the instrument God uses to make His truth steer the minds, hearts, and lives of His people. Through application, the Spirit shapes our thinking, our believing, and our behaving.

This application is more than a to-do list drawn from the ideas of the sermon; instead, it's the practical extension of the text's theme and thrust into the lives of the listeners. To offer application effectively, a pastor must possess a shepherd's love for and knowledge of his congregation, a heart-level openness to receive the Word personally, and the wisdom that can combine these two. Done well, this component of the sermon appeals to the conscience and penetrates the heart giving immediate relevance to the eternal truth.

One of church history's greatest preachers, commenting on another, confirms the necessity of application. The great scholar, theologian, and preacher, John Owen, was once asked by King Charles II why he went to hear the uneducated John Bunyan preach. He responded, 'I would willingly exchange my learning for the tinker's power of touching men's hearts.' Effective preaching is not merely the transfer of biblical truth, but the Spirit-empowered application of that truth to shape hearts.

---

12. Chapell, 199-200.

Go and Do Likewise

It's almost embarrassing to provide this meager introduction to expository preaching, but we would fail in our task to call you to something and not at least point you in the right direction. Our hope is that you would take these words as arrows that direct you to a treasure trove of resources that will complete the description we have only just begun.[13] But we offer this introduction because we share the convictions of John Stott when he writes: 'A low level of Christian living is due, more than anything else, to a low level of Christian preaching. If the church is to flourish again, there is a need for faithful, powerful, biblical preaching. God still urges his people to listen and his preachers to proclaim his word.'[14]

Despite what a fading and faltering congregation might think, this Word is critical for church revitalizations. As He has always done, God will use the Spirit-empowered exposition and application of His Word to bring fruit in once-arid spaces. The people may respond with snarls and scowls, but we must persevere in this labor to prepare and preach expository sermons. This preaching is a gift to the church. We must do more than merely talk from or about the Bible each week. We must go to the dry places of church revitalization and wield this instrument of God's life-giving work to cause His people to flourish.

---

13. We commend the books we have cited in this chapter as the best place to start.

14. John Stott, *Between Two Worlds* (Grand Rapids: Eerdmans, 1982), 22.

5

Faithful Preaching Over the Long-term

As we said from the outset, the necessity of supernatural endurance in pastoral ministry is a multifaceted topic, but our concern focuses in the area of preaching. We pray pastors will endure in evangelism, in pastoral care, in leading, in equipping, and in serving, but we're writing to encourage, exhort, and equip men to persevere in preaching. Despite the mountain of excellent books on preaching available today, we join the chorus of quality voices on the subject by contributing a harmonic tone of perseverance that is especially relevant for at least a few reasons.

The Challenges to Perseverance in Our Culture

First, perseverance is not a characteristic of our culture. Twenty-first century Western culture in general and American culture in particular are not often described as durable under pressure. The stereotypes are such common knowledge that we don't even need a source. Millennials (those born between 1980 and 2000) are widely described as 'needy and entitled.' They thirst for immediate gratification and crave constant entertainment through an ever-expanding array of media. They've been sheltered by overprotective parents, told they were as unique as a snowflake and as special as a butterfly, and in many ways, groomed for impatience. They don't want to wait for anything and every pastor under the age of thirty-nine belongs to this generation.

As much as we might nod along in agreement based on personal experience and anecdotal evidence, the social scientists continue to survey, study, and debate the accuracy of these descriptions. I'll wade out in the discussion far enough to say this description is accurate for millennials ... and for every other generation that has inhabited planet earth. It's a function of what the Bible calls *flesh*. It's not owing to our physical frame, but to our fallen-ness. I'll admit that certain manifestations of impatience from this younger generation are particularly annoying to me, but didn't our parents and grandparents express similar sentiments about us? Remember the 'back in my day ...' rants that made us roll our eyes as teenagers and young adults? Just because we're on the other side of the conversation doesn't make it novel.

Whether our culture is less inclined toward endurance than it used to be is a subject for a different book, but our point is that endurance has never been any human culture's forte. Twenty-first century America reflects the same impatience displayed when Abraham laid down with Hagar, Jacob demanded a blessing, Moses hit the rock, and David sent for Bathsheba. The call for perseverance in preaching is pertinent because pastors are human and humans lack patience.

Second, current cultural pressures have produced a level of expectation for preachers that often works against a commitment to faithful exposition. Judging by the crowds, the average evangelical churchgoer wants a preacher who is authentic, relatable, relevant, attentive to felt needs, and able to give practical application. Individual listeners will verbalize the list in slightly different ways, but at the core they value a style over the substance of faithful exposition. Even preachers with an understanding of and commitment to expository preaching are tempted to abandon it in favor of self-help talks lightly seasoned with Bible references in an effort to appeal to a contemporary audience. We push back against this trend in full awareness of how challenging it is.

Under normal circumstances the weight is heavy enough, but a majority of pastors will shepherd plateaued or declining congregations. According to recent research from Thom Rainer, the number of evangelical churches in this category is 65 per cent.[1] These are fields with hardened soil of complacency and thick weeds of worldliness. Most have not experienced a steady diet of weekly, faithful exposition in decades, and therefore are not inclined to ask for it or value it. Our churches need the fresh wind of revitalization, and it will come through pastors who persevere in the pulpit. It may not come rapidly, but we can be sure that the Word will accomplish its purpose.

After a decade of ministry to pastors in the trenches of these fields, I (Brian) know firsthand the struggle pastors – especially young ones – face without the perspective or

---

1. Thom Rainer, 'Dispelling the 80 Percent Myth of Declining Churches,' accessed 10-25-18 https://thomrainer.com/2017/06/dispelling-80-percent-myth-declining-churches/.

resolve necessary to endure in the pulpit ministry. Despite the biblical evidence for the centrality and necessity of consistent exposition, a tragic number of these evangelical churches in need of revitalization are dying or drifting due – in large part – to the absence of faithful, biblical preaching. Again, the situations are complex, and a host of reasons contribute to the decline, but the lack of preaching in these arid climates is primary.

Lest you think we're writing only for the small and struggling, we know that endurance in preaching is not restricted to weaker churches. In fact, some churches appear to be thriving based on the size of crowd but are producing emaciated disciples. It appears Willow Creek's now-infamous confessions in the 'Reveal' study have been largely ignored. They admitted that despite massive hordes of people, they were making very few genuine disciples.[2] But the lure of apparent success is so strong that they (and churches who follow their model) have made very few significant adjustments to their overall 'seeker-sensitive' strategy. Faithful exposition does not fit with those philosophical commitments, so even a cursory glance in their direction reveals a deficiency in preaching.

The numeric increases of these types of megachurches not only weaken the state of preaching in their gatherings, they cast a shadow on pastors and churches enamored by the glamor of growth. Thus, even pastors in philosophical alignment with our position on preaching often end up letting go of the rope. Like a baby needs milk or a plant needs

---

2. Greg Hawkins and Cally Parkinson, *Move* (Grand Rapids: Zondervan, 2011), 16.

water, all churches – big or small, strong or weak, growing or declining – need a steady diet of biblical exposition. The growing problem is that few of them have a palate for it, and thus, they refuse to ingest it. Even worse, they dismiss any who offer it on the menu.

Third, the continuing effects of our culture's obsession with entertainment require a renewed call to endure in preaching. Neil Postman reminds me of Balaam. You'll remember the latter as a pagan prophet God used to relay truth to His people in Numbers 22–24. Even though the Apostle Peter invokes the memory of Balaam to highlight false teachers who are out for personal gain, what can't be denied is that the man told the truth. Postman may be less familiar than Balaam to you. I'm certainly not trying to malign him, insinuate he was motivated by money, or speak about the status of his soul, but I see a strong resemblance in one way. The point of comparison for me is that, like Balaam, he was an outsider who uttered prophetic words of truth that God's people would be wise to heed. I can't say anything about him personally, but his insights about culture were profound and he's looking smarter every year.

Postman was an author, educator, and media ecologist who died in 2003. He wrote a number of books including *Amusing Ourselves to Death*, in which he warned about the negative effects of modern media and communication environments. He argued that the medium of communication, which include the structure, content, and instrument of delivery, irrevocably affects the message. And further, the use of technologies for entertainment has corrupted their use for serious communication. Take the television, for example. Because it is the source of endless hours of mindless entertainment, it cannot merely inform the mind. Instead, even serious information will be received through a lens of expectation that whatever is communicated ought to be entertaining. The method of communicating, therefore, is never merely an empty container or vehicle for the content.

Almost forty years ago, Postman warned that our growing obsession with entertainment would lead to a reduction of attention spans and an inability to think critically. Because laziness and consumerism are promoted and trumpeted, they will ultimately win the day and everything from news to politics to religion will suffer. Related to the news, the practice of laying the significant and the insignificant side-by-side will dull our sensitivity to what is actually important. Related to politics, we will value style over substance and celebrity over conviction. Could the 2016 presidential election have been a clearer vindication of his prophetic word? And most importantly related to religion, the avowed atheist predicted that faith communities would value entertainment over content.

Postman was right, we're amusing ourselves to death. In case you're not convinced, I offer one final, anecdotal piece of damning evidence courtesy of television from an occasion when a program placed the significant and the silly side-by-side in unforgettable fashion. The television company interrupted an evening talent competition show with a special announcement of the death of long-time senator John McCain (who had been an American POW during the Vietnam War, and was previously a two-time presidential candidate). The somber, reverential moment immediately evaporated when the 'regular programming' resumed and two shirtless, plump-bellied men wearing dolphin masks made 'music' by pressing a small air-pump against their respective, flabby midsections as they danced around a stage. Have mercy.

While I lament the degradation of our collective minds and sensitivities, this entertainment-addiction is taking a more serious and eternal toll in our churches. The value of the picture over the word is eroding our confidence in the act of preaching. This preference for the visual over and against the spoken weakens the preacher's resolve and the listener's commitment to work to receive the life-changing message of the Scripture. We're lulled into believing that 'learning' should be as easy as watching a television program or scrolling a social media feed. But thoughtful public discourse – i.e. preaching – requires work from all parties that is not only uncommon in our culture, but nearly completely devalued. Furthermore, the thirst for entertainment creates unhealthy expectations for the preaching event. Perhaps only subtly, but we expect the sermon to simulate an amusement park ride of emotional rises and falls that grabs and holds our attention while motivating us to reach for new heights. But the local church isn't Disney World. And preaching isn't *Flight of Passage*.

The Challenges to Perseverance in Every Culture

Well, I hope you're convinced that endurance in preaching is tough because our human nature, our church subculture, and our society are all working against us. But that's actually not the worst of it. The adversary, the devil, Satan himself and all his minions hate the proclamation of God's Word. From the Bible's third chapter to the very end, the evil one tries to hoodwink, bamboozle, confuse, bewilder, and dupe people to subvert God's authority and their confidence in His Word. Therefore, our fight to keep on preaching is not merely a mortal one. It is not merely a pushback against culture and the value-systems of an increasingly secular society. It's an all-out, spiritual war.

Without doubt, the horizon is dark and foreboding, but hope is not lost. The battle is neither new nor lost. Remember brothers, that the victory is ours in Christ. We are more than conquerors. This is not to say that we'll come out on top of every culture war or, in this case, steer the American people to embrace thoughtful public discourse. But we are assured that God's Word will accomplish God's exact purpose. So, we must preach.

Most scholars agree Paul's last surviving correspondence is the biblical book of Second Timothy. The life of this great missionary, church planter, evangelist, preacher, and slave of Christ was nearing an end when he wrote this deeply personal and theologically robust letter to his protégé. His words are intimate and inspired by God. His instruction is touching and timeless. His tone is raw and realistic. The short book urges a younger pastor to be strong and to fulfill his spiritual role no matter what comes against him. Every generation of pastors does well to hear and heed them. We offer this New Testament letter as the climactic and fundamental message of our book.

Paul wastes no time. After his customary opening and salutation, he expresses thanksgiving to God and moving affection for his brother and trainee in ministry. The tone quickly shifts from longing and gratitude to exhortation. He strikes the chords of endurance right out of the gate with a well-known imperative. 'I remind you to fan into flame the gift of God ...' (2 Tim. 1:6). Commentators are nearly-unanimous in viewing this gift, which was also mentioned by Paul in 1 Timothy 4:14, as Timothy's call to pastor and preach.

Thus, Paul is exhorting him to remember to 'fan it into flame.' The Greek word is a present, active, infinitive form of a verb that could be translated as 're-kindle' or 'kindle afresh.'[3] What a powerful and present word, brother pastor, that must continuously stoke the fires of zeal for our preaching ministry. Through our own spiritual apathy, ministry indifference, or even personal trial, the zeal to preach and shepherd will ebb and flow. Yet, we are accountable to God, the Giver of our gift, to steward this treasure well. Your struggle to maintain the emotional and spiritual energy to ascend the pulpit every week is neither new nor unique. God, who is rich in mercy, has not left us alone in this battle; He has given us His Spirit. While only some versions capitalize 'Spirit' in verse 7, we think they get it right. God has not merely given us an inner constitution to withstand; instead, we are indwelt by the Holy Spirit and so have His power, His love, and His self-control. This is not only consistent with the flow of this passage, but also the flow of the Pauline corpus and the New Testament as a whole. These virtues do not arise from ourselves but from God's work in us. Therefore, both the command and the power to obey it are ours. We must fan our gift into flame. We must do this by the power of God in us.

---

3. Joseph Thayer, *Thayer's Greek-English Lexicon of the New Testament* (Peabody, MA: Hendrickson, 2002), 37.

In typical Pauline fashion, he uses the connective word 'therefore' to build on the exhortation with more precision and focus. In 1:8-14, he drives home the call to endure. Using a negative command, he calls on Timothy to be steadfast in sharing the suffering of our Lord and His Apostle to the Gentiles. As we tried to make clear in Chapters 1 and 2, suffering is an essential aspect of the call to gospel ministry. Paul continues, Christ is our salvation, this gospel is our message, and this calling to preach is our responsibility and joy. We have been appointed by God for this 'holy calling' and we suffer not because of any neglect by, or failure of, God to protect His servants. The Apostle endured hardships for the sake of the elect by the sovereign purpose of God. Finally, Paul invites us, through the battlefield of hostility, the fog of apathy, and the valley of adversity, to follow him as he followed Christ.

Never one to shy away from confrontation, this letter by Paul exhibits a rawness that exceeds his other writings. He plainly reminds Timothy of specific examples of hostility that continue to occur in his ministry. The tides of opposition did not wane the longer he preached. In 4:14 he names one opponent, Alexander the coppersmith, who did great harm to him. And 'watch out,' he warns Timothy, 'this man will do the same to you because he strongly opposes our message.' The more passive assaults came as well. Paul mentions the turning away of 'all who are in Asia,' including Phygelus and Hermongenes (1:15), and the desertion of Demas (4:10). Even some who sat under the apostolic preaching ministry of Paul turned aside. This turning aside was not merely personal to Paul because it is a function of preaching in a sin-saturated world. He notes amidst the charge, to which we'll turn later, that many will abandon the truth in favor of a more palatable message. Lastly, the buffeting of adversity came from many sides. Based solely on this letter, we know that Paul faced loneliness, false teaching in the churches, other controversies in the church, physical maladies, and the ongoing fight against personal sin.

The Call to Persevere Supersedes Culture

Paul never pretends ministry will be anything other than this. He never baits Timothy with comfort only to switch it for suffering. Hostility, apathy, and adversity are common in every culture. With full awareness of what he has experienced and will continue to face, Paul gives the seminal charge in 2 Timothy 4:1-5:

> I charge you in the presence of God and of Christ Jesus, who is to judge the living and the dead, and by his appearing and his kingdom: preach the word; be ready in season and out of season; reprove, rebuke, and exhort, with complete patience and teaching. For the time is coming when people will not endure sound teaching, but having itching ears they will accumulate for themselves teachers to suit their own passions, and will turn away from listening to the truth and wander off into myths. As for you, always be sober-minded, endure suffering, do the work of an evangelist, fulfill your ministry.

If you don't already know these words well, I hope you're only just now training for ministry because this is our essential charge. Brother pastor, this paragraph summarizes the stewardship we are given more clearly and succinctly than perhaps any other.

This power-packed-paragraph contains nine imperatives for Timothy, and, by extension through the Spirit's inspiration, to all Christian preachers. First, preach the Word. It's at the front of the list for a reason. As I hope you've seen by now, we submit that this task is primary. We are heralds of the sacred Word from God. The next four commands display the primacy of this one as they explain and expound upon it. Second, be ready all the time. The implication is that we must be prepared to preach.

Then the next three exhortations pile on: reprove, rebuke, and exhort. The first two of these have very similar meanings and they convey negative functions of the ministry of the Word. While similar, MacArthur insightfully distinguishes between them saying, 'Reproving may have more to do with the mind,' but '[r]ebuke, on the other hand, may have more to do with the heart.'[4] Based on Paul's words in the prior section of 2 Timothy, we are not surprised to find reproof among the preacher's task because it is a function of the inscripturated Word. These aim for the corrective nature of the Word to confront sin and to call for repentance. The final imperative in the narrow vein of preaching is exhort. The root of this term is the same one used for the Holy Spirit in John 14 and 16. He is the *Parakletos* and we are to *parakaleo*. We are to extend the ministry of the Spirit through the proclamation of the Word to comfort, build up, and strengthen believers.

The final four imperatives extend beyond the pulpit capturing a more holistic sense of the pastor's ministry. Sober-mindedness is a quality of spiritual leaders that pertains to alcohol but extends past it to all areas of life.

4. John MacArthur, '2 Timothy' in *The MacArthur New Testament Commentary* (Chicago: Moody, 1995), 177.

The person who is described this way is 'moderate, well-balanced, calm, careful, steady, and sane.'[5] He is filled with spiritual and moral earnestness. We'll save the seventh command for last and note, 'do the work of an evangelist.' Never forget that our gospel proclamation is not confined to the pulpit. We must generously, liberally, scatter the seed of the Word. In summation, 'fulfill your ministry.' Do what God has called you to do.

Every imperative is important and all deserve their due, but our focus is limited. Thus, we come finally to the seventh one on Paul's list and the one at the top of ours at this point in this book: 'endure suffering.' This phrase translates a single word in the Greek: *kakopatheson*. The word most plainly means to suffer or undergo hardship. Like all the words on this list, it's in the aorist tense and the active voice. The aorist tense, which often indicates past action, clearly does not communicate that enduring suffering is a past activity for Timothy. Instead, the aorist tense, applied to an imperative as it is here, relates future action that is unspecified or unlimited. As the active voice conveys, this 'activity' is expected to continue. Hence, almost every English translation includes the word 'endure.' Let the mini-Greek lesson solidify this truth in your minds: suffering is anticipated, *and* endurance is required.

Perhaps some are reading this book and wondering if they can scale the platform stairs another week, stand behind the pulpit, and proclaim the excellencies of God's Word with passion. Yes, by the power of the Spirit, you can. And by the

---

5. William Hendrickson, 'I-II Timothy' in *New Testament Commentary*. Fourth Printing. (Grand Rapids: Baker Academic, 2007), 122.

calling of God, you must. Paul concludes the exhortation with self-reflection. He tells us to do something that, by God's grace, he has been able to do. 'I have fought the good fight. I have finished the race. I have kept the faith.' He doesn't boast of being the stronger fighter, the faster runner, or the better preacher. No, he is simply one who persevered.

Don't misunderstand, this exhortation does not mean that a pastor must preach every sermon, every week for as long as he is physically able. Instead, the call is to run the marathon of ministry consistently over the long-term. The thrust of our encouragement is not to carry the burden of ministry alone or to ignore the reasonable limits of our human frailty, but to persevere in carrying the portion entrusted to us. Our assignment is lighter in the short-run than we want to admit and heavier in the long-run than we want to accept. We are not under pressure to preach an all-time great sermon every week; we are tasked with providing a steady diet of faithful sermons. James Boice is credited with saying that we usually overestimate what we can do in a year, but underestimate what can be accomplished in ten. This axiom applies well to the pulpit ministry. To borrow a baseball analogy, our congregations will benefit more from a lifetime of singles and doubles than from an inconsistent pattern of isolated homeruns followed by lots of swings-and-misses.

You're not Jesus. You're not even a preacher-version of Superman. You're an ordinary human with God-given responsibility and power. You can and you must stand up under it. The road will not be easy. If you preach the Word faithfully, you're sure to face hills of hostility, valleys of apathy, and potholes of adversity. Endurance is possible because God commands and then empowers it.

Part 3

Preaching with Your Feet to the Fire

6

PREACHING THROUGH HOSTILITY

You may have heard about my (Brian) church story. The first five years were brutal. I went to pastor a Southern Baptist Church of thirty elderly people on the southside of Louisville, Kentucky. The church was in financial shambles and about two to three years from closing. The church hired me at a salary I later found out they could not pay for longer than six months. There were three different efforts to get me fired in the first five years. The first attempt happened three short months into my ministry there by a staff member I inherited who boasted of getting my predecessor fired and tried to do the same with me.

The second firing attempt was at the two-and-a-half-year mark over trying to find the 580 members on the rolls who had not been to church in over ten years. They tried to remove me while I was on vacation. The third firing attempt was at the five-year mark – which ultimately led to an exodus of 25 per cent of my congregation, some of whom had come in the previous five years and had become dear friends. When the smoke cleared, I was beat up, discouraged and ready to leave. When asked why I stayed, I looked back and saw two reasons: First, I sensed God would not take us through all that and then abandon us. There were evidences of God's grace and work in the midst of the hostility. Second, I was haunted by the words of Hebrews 13:17: 'Obey your leaders and submit to them, for they are keeping watch over your souls, as those who will have to give an account. Let them do this with joy and not with groaning, for that would be of no advantage to you.' I realized I will give an account for every soul under my care, even those who don't like me very much. So, I stayed. And some of the hostile members stayed also. It was in year six where God in His power and grace turned the ship that led our church to change course and flourish.

The church grew numerically and, more importantly, spiritually. We affirmed a plurality of pastors and deacons where those who served in these biblical offices knew their Scriptural role and excelled in it. We saw conversions from the neighborhood. We saw our multi-generational-but-all-white congregation begin to grow in ethnic diversity. Refugees from the community began to come to the church. We raised up pastors and missionaries and sent them out. And most significantly, the angry, scowling faces I saw when I looked out while preaching every Sunday changed. Those who were once hostile to me began to trust me. They grew to love me and I them. And they grew to accept my preaching and even grew to love the preached Word more. I'm so glad I stayed and even more I am glad many of those who were hostile to me stayed. For it laid the ground work for a sovereign and powerful God to do this stunning redemptive work in the lives of a young, broken pastor and discouraged, hurting people.

Preaching through Hostility

The hostility I faced in the first five years was felt every week when I preached. It is not an exaggeration to say that for years I preached to angry, scowling faces. One reason for this was the enormous distrust the church had for the pastoral office as a result of a thirty-five-year pattern of two to three-year pastorates. Another reason, however, was the way I chose to preach was different than what they had previously experienced. I came to a seventy-five-year-old church who had never heard an expository sermon. Their steady diet of preaching for over half a century was very typical for a Southern Baptist Church – evangelistic topical preaching with a strong influence from the Billy Graham Crusades.

When I came to the church, I began preaching expository sermons through books of the Bible. It was not received well. People thought what I was doing was more of a Bible Study, and not preaching. I believed this was the best way to embrace God's design to breathe life into a church – through His Word being preached verse by verse. As I frustrated some members, God began to bring others desiring to hear God's Word through expository sermons. As a result, the first five years was a slow steady combination of winning current members with this form of preaching, drawing in others from outside the church who wanted this kind of preaching, and at the same time frustrating a few others who eventually left because of it.

By year five, 85 per cent of the pastoral committee who hired me had either died or left frustrated with my preaching in particular. The key member of the committee who got me an interview initially left after three years. Upon her exit, she wrote me a letter. She explained that she left because of the way I preached. I had chosen to preach from a manuscript because I wanted to be careful in those early years about what I said and didn't say. I committed myself to preach with a manuscript well. I'll be the first to acknowledge I needed to grow to engage the congregation better as I sought to preach from manuscripts. Those early years were frustrating for me in part because I was a young preacher trying to figure out who I was as a preacher – which every young pastor needs to figure out. I was convinced that God's Word linked with the Spirit of God was enough to build a healthy church – even through a young inexperienced preacher. So, through all the adversity and hostility, I kept preaching.

But it was hard. Really hard. However, in God's kind providence I realized it was through this hostility where I learned the biblical formula to sustain a preaching ministry in a hostile environment and even bear fruit in it. The formula is simple and yet profound – preach and stay.

Preach and Stay

The biblical formula to survive and bear fruit in the hostility of church revitalization is to *preach and stay*. Before we consider this formula, we need to be aware of two other common preaching strategies that exist in many church revitalization contexts that are harmful and do not bring lasting spiritual life to a dying church.

The first harmful preaching strategy is *preach and leave*. I watch many pastors, who share the convictions outlined in this book, go into a struggling church and preach faithfully. They preach the Bible with all their heart. They give themselves to study and prayer. They are committed to expository preaching. But they quickly grow impatient. They assume that an implication of God's Word being powerful is that it will bring change quickly. Out of frustration and unmet expectations they leave for the next church they feel will be different.

The other harmful preaching strategy is *don't preach, but stay*. This represents the other side that is committed to stay and be patient but does not feel the Word of God through expository preaching is the answer to bring life to a struggling church. In this scenario pastors either preach topical, lighthearted sermons, not wanting to offend, or, even worse feel no confidence in the role preaching plays to bring life back to a dying church. Instead, gimmicks, pragmatism, and entertainment become the trusted quick-fix strategy. The end goal is to try and make everyone happy.

Unfortunately, both these methods of preaching in revitalization do not bear fruit and are even harmful to the flock. The biblical formula to preach through hostility is to preach and stay.

Preach

As already mentioned in Chapter 5, one of the clearest commands in the New Testament is Paul's exhortation to

Timothy, then a young pastor, in the last letter on record that Paul wrote before his death:

> I charge you in the presence of God and of Christ Jesus, who is to judge the living and the dead, and by his appearing and his kingdom: preach the word; be ready in season and out of season; reprove, rebuke, and exhort, with complete patience and teaching. For the time is coming when people will not endure sound teaching, but having itching ears they will accumulate for themselves teachers to suit their own passions, and will turn away from listening to the truth and wander off into myths. As for you, always be sober-minded, endure suffering, do the work of an evangelist, fulfill your ministry (2 Tim. 4:1-5).

Paul's command to Timothy reveals the formula to build the church, even a dying one – preach the Word. The clarity of this command comes in the details that surround it:

- What – I charge you to preach the Word (vv. 1-2)
- When – In season and out of season (v. 2)
- How – Reprove, rebuke, and exhort with great patience and instruction (v. 2)
- Why – A time will come where they won't want it (vv. 3-4)

The formula is sealed with the exhortations that follow, 'As for you, always be sober-minded, endure suffering, do the work of an evangelist, fulfill your ministry' (v. 5). Paul leaves no doubt what the task is for Timothy as well as for every faithful pastor in the present day: 'Preach the Word ... while always being sober-minded, and fulfilling your ministry knowing there will be suffering in this task you must endure.' Paul, then, implies that the calling and task of a faithful pastor is to preach the Word, which often must be done within an environment of hostility.

Stay

There are many pastors who preach faithfully. There are several of those pastors who will do so boldly in a hostile environment. However, fewer of these pastors will endure the suffering and difficulty of doing it for years. And yet the full biblical formula is to preach *and stay*. Paul demonstrates this crucial piece at the end of his letter to the Corinthians and gives two reasons why he cannot come to them just yet:

> I will visit you after passing through Macedonia, for I intend to pass through Macedonia, and perhaps I will stay with you or even spend the winter, so that you may help me on my journey, wherever I go. For I do not want to see you now just in passing. I hope to spend some time with you, if the Lord permits. But I will stay in Ephesus until Pentecost, for a wide door for effective work has opened to me, and there are many adversaries (1 Cor. 16:5-9).

Paul desires to go to the Corinthians, but he explains to them two important reasons why he must stay in Ephesus.

The first reason Paul stays is *Paul's work is not yet done.* Paul had other plans but changed them as he realized God had opened a wide door for effective work where he already was. The Apostle desired to see the Corinthians and had plans to go and stay for a lengthy time with them, but God had other plans. So Paul stayed on in Ephesus to continue the work he started. There was still more for him to do.

The second reason Paul stays is *the presence of many adversaries.* So often pastors conclude the presence of adversaries and the hostility that accompanies these adversaries is the evidence that it is time to leave and go to the next ministry post. Paul functions on a completely different paradigm. Paul concludes it is the presence of many adversaries that demonstrates to him he is to stay.

So then, the biblical formula to survive, even thrive, in a preaching ministry that faces hostility is to preach the Word and stay. Pastors are to trust that the Word will build the church, provided that they stay long enough and preach persistently enough to give time for God to work. If pastors will preach and stay, there will exist the prospect of snarls and scowls turning to attentive hearers and joyful doers of the Word.

By God's grace, I stayed long enough to see this kind of spiritual fruit. I persevered to see the hostility turn to joy. After the ship turned in our church at the six-year mark, I looked back and learned five key lessons about preaching through hostility.

Five Lessons from Preaching and Staying
Had I preached and left, I would have missed these lessons. Had I compromised my efforts to preach expository sermons, I would have missed the fruit. And yet, I preached and stayed. In doing so, I learned these five key principles that will help a pastor preaching in a hostile context keep preaching and remain steadfast.

First, determine whether you really believe the Word builds the church. Many young pastors go into a struggling dying church and declare they believe the Word of God builds the church. Then, they pastor and preach like they believe the exact opposite. Pastors in their first church often lament their frustration that this needs to change, this part of the church is a disaster, and mad they can't change anything. Some, out of frustration, try to change a lot in the first couple of years and get fired. And, don't know why.

Pastors must resolve the most important change that needs to come into our churches immediately upon our arrival. That is, what comes from the pulpit. A pastor who really believes the Word builds the church over a long period of time doesn't ignore the other frustrations that need to change. But if pastors desire to be consistent with the belief that the Word builds the church, then they should resolve to focus most on their preaching ministry and loving those people who are there when they begin their ministry.

Second, listen to those who don't like your preaching ... and why? In the early years, I thought I was the patient one. I was enduring through the criticisms, judgments, and actions to remove me. I was being the bigger, more faithful person. I was the one preaching my heart out to the scowls in the crowd. As the years have passed, I have realized in a lot of ways that it was the other way around. These long-time faithful saints, wounded by previous pastors for decades, were being patient with me. Specifically, they were being patient with me as I grew as a preacher.

Betty, an eighty-five-year-old long-term member and widow, used to criticize my preaching in the early years. She was the only one who came to me to tell me she didn't like my preaching and why. I dismissed what she said. As I sought to grow for the next eight years, she proved to be right. As I grew as a preacher, I suddenly realized I had made changes that she suggested years before. She loves to hear me tell that story. Even more, she loves to hear me preach now. She regularly greets me with tears after a sermon because of the way the Word ministered to her weary soul. She and others were patient with me, especially with my preaching. Listen to those who don't like your preaching. Preach and listen with great patience and instruction. Don't underestimate the patience they are showing you. It might be that those God specifically uses to criticize you will help you grow the most as a preacher.

Third, remember the Word never returns void – even through scowls. I remember those early years were so hard to preach. I lacked confidence in my preaching. Few ever brought a Bible and used it. Many sat with folded arms and angry faces. I remember, as this hostile place began to wear on me, I printed and taped a message on the top of the pulpit for me to stare at when I would preach. The message said this:

> You don't preach for the praise of man, but to declare the truth of God's Word. It is enough and a worthy, noble work to preach God's Word even if it is not received by the hearers.

If you can't find the joy in God's Word being proclaimed regardless of how your hearers respond, you won't last long preaching in a hostile, dying church. This is a classic reason many pastors leave. We must trust that God is at work using His Word in our preaching in numerous ways, even when we can't see it. Our calling is to preach and endure. We leave the results to God. It is not an accident that Paul follows the command of 'Preach the word' with 'endure hardship' so to 'fulfill your ministry' (2 Tim. 4:1-5). Preaching through hostility leads us on the road to fulfilling our ministry. God's Word never returns void – even through scowls.

Fourth, embrace a supportive, but unimpressed evaluation of your preaching. Pastors often seek affirmation and encouragement by surrounding themselves with those who think they are the greatest preacher, most compassionate counselor, and strongest leader. In doing so, they avoid those who have less flattering thoughts of them. Instead, the solution is to have a supportive, but unimpressed evaluation of your preaching. This role is best played by a faithful pastor's wife. I know this because I have a wife who is very supportive, and very unimpressed with me.

- *Supportive*: It is our wives who know us better than anyone. They know our struggles, faults, inadequacies, and sins. And yet they have unshakable support, love, affirmation and care for us. They are there and with us through the most painful conflicts, greatest betrayals, and worst sermons. In an atmosphere of hostility, every pastor needs this kind of support.

- *Unimpressed:* Unwavering support of a wife is of great value to a pastor, but one of the worst roles for a pastor's wife to play is to view her husband and his ministry with rose-colored glasses. The blind spots in a pastor's life, ministry, and preaching are most clearly and carefully observed by his intuitive, 'supportive, but unimpressed' wife. A pastor's wife that is impressed with her husband will not help him see the areas of pride and self-deceit in his heart that show up in conversations at home. A pastor's wife impressed with her husband's preaching will not objectively listen to him preach for the purpose to help him grow as a preacher. A pastor's wife impressed with her husband's gifts for ministry will be tempted to overlook those consistent criticisms that come from credible people in the church.

When preaching in a hostile environment, every pastor needs unwavering support, and yet someone who can help him evaluate the harsh words that come with hostility and discern what needs to be received or discarded. A pastor's wife so often can play this essential role, but not every pastor's wife can. If not his wife, every pastor needs to find that 'supportive, but unimpressed' evaluation of his ministry when preaching through hostility.

Fifth, know there's nothing like a congregation who grows hungry for the Word. One reason Paul instructs Timothy with 'Preach the Word in season and out of season with great patience and instruction' is that he knows those people over time will be changed by that Word. My first five years were brutal. All the fights, conflicts, scowls when preaching, folded arms in the pews, attacks in the community, and firing attempts in the early years have all made our church that much more a sweeter place now. It is hard to describe the feeling of seeing someone hear the Word and respond with tears of hope where someone once sat and scowled. It is so meaningful to be greeted by Betty after the service with a big hug and an encouraging word about how the sermon was helpful – when she used to use that moment to criticize.

Imagine a church where very few even brought a Bible, to now every time I direct our people to a verse in the passage, I see this downward head motion in unison. Because of the Lord's work in such a hard, hostile place, it has made this church the sweetest place to preach. There is nothing like a congregation who over time grows hungry for the Word. I assure you that there is not the same satisfaction when you inherit an eager healthy congregation as there is when you preach in a dying church to scowls and hostility and God, through His Word over the course of years, breathes life back into that church.

Therefore, persevere in your preaching, pastors! It is the means by which God will build His church. Then stay. Stay so you will see the spiritual fruit manifest from your preaching. Stay to see this work through. Stay to see how God chooses to bring life back into His church.

7

PREACHING THROUGH APATHY

Brian's story moves me (James) every time I hear it. The fact that he celebrated fifteen years of ministry at Auburndale this past year despite the initial opposition, the attempts to fire him, and the extended period without a vacation is nothing short of miraculous. An ordinary man would have folded in despair, started a fight in anger, or at least walked away to a greener field. As he was careful to admit, Brian is very much ordinary, but by God's extraordinary power, he stayed. I begin with that admission because in ways this chapter lacks the excitement and drama of the last. No stand-offs, showdowns, or theatrics.

I have not labored in the most difficult field. I have never felt abandoned or alone. I have never wondered if I was going to be paid. I have not been beaten or ridiculed. I have not been fired and forced to leave. I have not lost my wife. Yet, persevering at my post has not been easy. I would describe my trial as more like the nag of a dripping faucet than a rushing river. I have faced no tsunami of opposition, but the smaller waves of criticism just never stop. No individual wave is enough to overwhelm, but they *just never stop*. But I'm getting ahead of myself. Before telling a part of my story, let me remind you of the first group of believers in Corinth.

Chaos in Corinth

You think your church has issues? That church was an unmitigated disaster. They were sharply divided into factions based on allegiances to different teachers. They didn't have a good grasp of the gospel. They were ashamed of the cross. They lacked confidence in the preaching of the Word. They didn't understand the nature of Christian ministry. They were filled with pride. They exercised their Christian freedom in ways that harmed one another. They allowed, indulged in, and even celebrated all manner of immorality, particularly sexual immorality. They took one another to court to settle disputes. Congregational worship routinely descended into chaos. They over-indulged on wine from the Lord's table to the point of leaving none for the late-comers. They used spiritual gifts like weapons against one another. They doubted the fact and significance of the resurrection. And these are only the matters Paul addresses in one letter. Suffice it to say, it was bedlam.

As Paul addresses this three or four-year-old church concerning a myriad of struggles, he provides a mountain of lasting encouragement for pastors. Perhaps primarily, there is an overarching reassurance emerging from the fact that Paul had reason to write the letter in the first place. If this church, which was planted and pastored by the great missionary and Apostle to the Gentiles, could decline so sharply and quickly after his departure, we shouldn't expect perfection in our congregations. These flocks over which God has granted us to lead, feed, protect, and care are comprised of sheep. At some point every one of them is vulnerable, weak-willed, lacking in wisdom, given to impulses, and fickle. And by the way, even though we fulfill the role of under-shepherd, we are, at the same time, sheep. The propensities to spiritual weakness live in us, too.

Zooming in to each portion of the letter, we find implied and corollary instructions for pastors as Paul fires away at the various issues raised by Chloe's people and by the Corinthians' questions. For my purpose in writing now, I draw your attention to his correction of their quarrelsomeness and cliquishness in Chapter 3. Paul takes aim at these cancerous characteristics through the first several chapters of the letter and in this passage he addresses one underlying cause for it: factions based on preference for certain teachers. He raised this issue in 1:12 and restated it in 3:4 as part of a rhetorical question. This whole enterprise, Paul argues, is foolishness because even the greatest teachers are merely servants. Everything – the church, the servants, and the fruitfulness of any ministry – belongs to God. Visible ministry effectiveness, then, is granted by God and not necessarily an indicator of faithfulness on the part of the servant. Paul warns that regardless of outward appearances in the present, the genuine quality of ministerial labor will be revealed on the last day in the fires of God's judgment. Therefore, don't attach yourselves to slaves, but maintain allegiance to God.

Again, this passage is most directly aimed at tribalism in the church. Paul is grieved by their bickering and one-upmanship. The church is God's; it's not Paul's or Apollos' or

Cephas'. The clearest and most straightforward application, therefore, is a call for unity. His argument for this unity, though, is grounded in a proper understanding of the church and of Christian ministry. He contends in verses 5 through 9 that gospel ministers are 'God's fellow workers' and that each church is 'God's field, God's building.'

He carries these two analogies forward into verses 10-15 explaining that gospel ministry is nothing more than a continuation of the building project began in Christ. The privilege to join this work as a builder is a 'grace,' or undeserved gift from God. Thus, we are responsible to steward this charge faithfully knowing that, in the short-term, only God will know the true value of our labor. In the end, however, this truth will be disclosed and some who have appeared like master builders on earth will 'be saved, but only as through fire.'

The conclusion of this small section is a warning for builders. Using a plural 'you,' Paul explains that the congregation is God's temple in which dwells the Holy Spirit. While he makes a similar point by applying this metaphor to individuals in Chapter 6, here he speaks of God's ownership of and indwelling presence in them as a collective. The point is to set-up the warning of verse 17: 'If anyone destroys God's temple, God will destroy him.' The warning is most directly aimed at the church members who are 'destroying' the church through divisiveness. But the corollary warning for pastors is not missed. We will answer to God, and not to man, for the discharge of our ministry duties.

What has Corinth to do with Bardstown?

In many ways, nothing at all. Bardstown, in Kentucky, is a million miles from the ancient city of Corinth. Corinth was a key commercial, political, and cultural center in the first-century Roman Empire. It was located at a crucial spot of convergence for the major land and sea routes of ancient Greece and was a strategic connection point between the mainland and the more mountainous southern region. The sea squeezed in from both sides, so Corinth sat on an isthmus with ports to both the east and west. Therefore, this city was an intersection point for travelers moving north and south by land and travelers going east and west by sea. Population estimates are notoriously varied for ancient cities, but most agree Corinth was huge. Some guess it was as high as 750,000. The constant stream of travelers from every direction and the massive population brought cultural influences from all sides.

Convenience wasn't the only reason travelers came, however. As the capital of Greece, the seat for Roman administration in the region, and the host of the Isthmian Games, thousands came each year for social, political, economic, and entertainment interests. Add to these factors, Corinth was an extraordinarily pagan city with pervasive sexual immorality. The city accommodated the worship of many Greek gods including, primarily, Aphrodite, the goddess of love. As is often the case, 'vice and religion flourished side by side.'[1] The Corinthians became famous in the Roman Empire for pushing the boundaries of sexual immorality. As Fee summarizes: 'All this evidence suggests that Paul's Corinth was at once the New York, Los Angeles, and Las Vegas of the ancient world.'[2]

---

1. Gordon D. Fee, 'The First Epistle to the Corinthians' in *New International Commentary on the New Testament* (Grand Rapids, Eerdmans, 1987), 2.

2. Ibid., 3.

By human standards, the church at Corinth could also boast. As Luke records in Acts 18, this congregation was started by the world's most famous Christian missionary, the Apostle Paul. He planted the church during his second missionary journey, most likely arriving in the fall of A.D. 50. Unlike his normal pattern up to that point, he spent about eighteen months investing in this new church. In addition to Paul, this first congregation was also led, at least to some degree, by Aquila and Priscilla, and later by Apollos. That's a strong base.

By contrast, Bardstown (pop. 13,227) is one of the most beautiful small towns in America.[3] We can't boast of being any kind of commercial, political, or cultural hub. Located forty miles south of Louisville and sixty miles southwest of Lexington, it sits on a semi-major state road connecting major Interstate arteries, but no one would call this town a hub for major travel. It can tout a few tourist sites and draws thousands of visitors each year, but it's certainly not a major travel destination. As the thirtieth largest town in Kentucky, Bardstown is big enough to have decent infrastructure and a few nice places to eat, but again, it's no rival to ancient Corinth.

When it comes to spiritual matters, this town is as dark as any other. Cultural Christianity is pervasive along with numerous forms of idolatry. It wouldn't take much investigation to find all fifteen works of the flesh from Galatians 5:19-21 manifested around here. Yet, most people in this context won't be out bragging about it. The town is squarely in a 'red state' and the majority of people outwardly

---

3. Rand McNally assigned this designation to Bardstown in 2012.

value societal norms for morality that accord with Judeo-Christian ideals.

Another point of contrast is that while Corinth had zero churches when Paul came to town, Bardstown has many. Following the Revolutionary War, this was the first center of Roman Catholicism west of the Appalachian Mountains and home to the first diocese on the western frontier in 1808. Less than a quarter of the population identifies as Roman Catholic today as Evangelical Protestants surpassed them by a few hundred adherents in the last twenty years and now have four times as many congregations. A small percentage of the population identifies with other groups, like Mainline Protestants and Black Protestants, but the single largest category (45 per cent) is comprised of those who claim no religious affiliation. It's not quite Corinth, but this town has plenty of lostness.

This background may seem excessive, but it sets the context for my ministry in this town. The deep trenches of cultural Catholicism and the recent growth of Evangelical churches in the last two decades are important. Moving in even more closely, I moved to this town to pastor Parkway Baptist Church in the summer of 2010. Parkway started in 1996 when a group of around 200 people left another church together. That story is an interesting one, but someone else will have to tell it because I wasn't there.

What happened prior to 1996 aside, the record of what happened in the next twelve years is clear. The church grew rapidly in membership and in weekly attendance, topping 500 in average weekly attendance in 2001 and surging above 800 in 2008. They celebrated dozens of baptisms and membership transfers, adding more than 100 members in each year from 2001 to 2008. Their methodology followed the attractional model made popular by Willow Creek and Saddleback. By all accounts, this was a thriving and healthy church.

Controversy that is beyond the scope of this book led to the departure of the church's only pastor in December 2008. When I arrived eighteen months later, things were holding steady, but the signs of deteriorating health were beginning to show. According to a Church Health Survey,[4] taken in 2009, the congregation was at least marginally unhealthy according to all six indicators: evangelism, discipleship, fellowship, ministry, prayer, and worship. As I considered the potential of God leading me to shepherd these people, it was obvious that the future would not look like the past. Their value system was grounded in a man-centered paradigm for ministry that I am convinced is patently dangerous for a church's long-term viability. While the larger story deserves to be told, focusing on the preaching ministry will reveal the situation and carry the theme of this book forward.

I preached my first sermon as pastor on July 11, 2010 from Philippians 1:1-11. On the surface, most everything seemed normal. The sermon lasted a few minutes longer than their custom, but the biggest shock was the announcement that we'd be back in Philippians 1 the following Sunday. For the first time in the church's fourteen-year history, we invested eleven consecutive weeks working verse-by-verse through a single book of the Bible. Then, to the surprise of many, we turned to the book of Joshua, and hit repeat. We studied the

---

4. Parkway worked with the Lawless Group to complete their Church Health Survey. You can find more information about this group and the survey at thelawlessgroup.com.

Prologue of John's Gospel during December of that year. At the start of the new year, and to the chagrin of many, we launched a new series in Acts. After investing the first quarter of the year working verse-by-verse from 1:1 to 8:8, we shifted to the Old Testament book of Malachi. And on and on we've gone for the last eight-plus years.

The difference is not merely that we've worked through nine New Testament books, five Old Testament books, and portions of several others, although that has been different. The expository approach to the pulpit ministry stood in stark contrast to the diet of topical preaching they had been accustomed to. Instead of crafting congregational worship to make it easy for casual attenders to watch and enjoy, we began building moments for believers to participate in all aspects of the service. This includes active listening to the proclamation of God's Word through concentration and effort. Expository preaching includes (as we tried to show in chapter 4) the faithful and careful explanation of a biblical text that emerges from a historical, literary, and biblical context. This method lays enormous demands on the preacher in his study and on the listener in the preaching event.

As the title of this chapter infers, the dominant reaction to my preaching ministry here has been apathy. A few folks have expressed mild forms of hostility, but the most common displeasure has manifested as laziness, lethargy, and indifference. Some people place little to no value on biblical preaching out of ignorance, but more often genuine believers lack the spiritual maturity to appreciate and absorb the meat of God's Word. This apathy has fueled three basic responses. A great many people have been shaped by the biblical exposition and are growing in their love and appreciation for the Word. Others have somewhat quietly walked away to join other churches. The final group have remained and continue to voice persistent criticism. I hesitate to use the word persecution, but not the word suffering. For a shepherd to watch the slow decline of attendance or hear the drip of criticism takes an enormous toll.

I referenced attendance numbers above, which when set beside our most recent averages will tell a story. As of late September 2018, our average weekly attendance in congregational worship for this year is 433. That's a difference of nearly 400! Relocations due to job transfers can explain a few of those, but most have been people staying in Bardstown and deciding to worship somewhere else. Yes, some left because of relational conflict or ministry-related matters, but a large number listed my preaching as a key determiner in their exit. Ouch.

As hard as it is to watch them leave and know it's my fault, having disgruntled members stay is not much better. Eight years into my ministry here, I am still confronted with criticism of my preaching from new sources nearly every month. New criticism comes despite the fact that it is virtually the same as it's been for almost a decade. If you preach regularly, you're certainly familiar with the Monday morning blues. That ominous cloud of discouragement, guilt, or shame that comes after pouring out your heart and soul in the pulpit on Sunday only to walk away with the sinking feeling that you just might be the worst pastor/preacher on the planet. Now imagine having that insecurity confirmed week after week, month after month, year after year, by people who will vocalize their displeasure in your sermons.

This is not to say that I have not received encouragement. Scores of people consistently affirm me, my preaching, and more importantly, the work of God through the preaching of the Word. God is building His Kingdom and He is doing a good work at Parkway. Hundreds of people are being established by the ministry of the Word. Scores of people encourage me at nearly every turn. This field is not the hard soil of Isaiah's day, but it's hard enough. The temptation to fixate on the one word of criticism is strong, even when it is surrounded by a dozen words of appreciation. I can logically explain why this is foolish and dangerous, but it takes the work of the Spirit in me to overcome it. This may not be the most difficult field, but it's not easy. In fact, it's nearly broken me more than once.

This danger is deadly because it drains the joy out of ministry through pinholes. It may lack the drama of a showdown or the intensity of a frontal assault, but the constant drip of criticism will weary a man to the point of submission. The resolve to persevere evaporates slowly under the weight of insecurity because of a deadly concoction of unrealistic expectation and pride lurking within every (or nearly every) pastor. The mistaken notion that some version of ministry success awaits us will sprout seedlings of jealousy and contempt when those prospects don't materialize. The pendulum then swings to the other side of pride, from self-glory to self-pity. Our sense of failure from within is stoked by the brands of criticism igniting embers of discouragement. The fire doesn't burn bright enough or hot enough at first to attract attention, so the coals smolder unnoticed.

I would liken it to slowly boiling a frog or filling a backpack with small pebbles, one at a time. If you want to weigh me down to the point of exhaustion, don't put a boulder in my backpack. I'll realize it's too heavy before I even try and give up. Add a pebble or two to my backpack every week and the change in weight will be imperceptible. Before I know it, the weight is too much to bear. There are no enemies to oppose or battles to fight; instead, apathy to faithful preaching leads some people to a different pasture and others to slowly slip away. No single loss or isolated cutting comment is enough to topple the man, but the accumulation wears him down to the breaking point. The greatest danger for a man at that moment is to walk away in search of a new backpack. Sometimes he finds a new field of ministry and other times he walks away from the pulpit dejected. Yes, there are times for ministry transitions, but the burden of an apathetic congregation ought not be the catalyst for it.

Brothers, I write these words from beside you on the road. I have not completed the race and I'm not wearing the victor's crown. This struggle is still very much in the present for me. I can commiserate with you and, by God's grace, offer words of hope for you. Let's go back to 1 Corinthians 3.

Encouragement for Enduring through Apathy

By God's providence, in the months that preceded my coming to Parkway, I was team-teaching through 1 Corinthians. One of the texts assigned to me was 3:5-17.

As I look back at my notes, I applied the text to the congregation by exhorting us toward maturity in regard to unity. I tried to honor Paul's intention in writing it and still think that's the most appropriate way to preach this text. However, I have run back to this text many times over the past few years and found several key applications that are implied and important for pastors serving an apathetic congregation.

First, you're not God's gift to the Church. Paul was a planter, Apollos was a waterer, and neither of them was 'anything.' They were instruments for God's garden work in the Corinthian field. In the same way that the rake gets no credit for the harvest of vegetables in your garden, the preacher deserves none for the harvest growing from his sermon. Before we wobble out of balance, allow Paul's words to bring us back into alignment. The Apostle Paul was not God's gift to the Church. He was one radically-converted, specifically-equipped, Spirit-empowered man. At the end of the day, he was not better than Apollos or John Chrysostom or George Whitefield or Charles Spurgeon or John Piper or you.

Brothers and sisters deserve appropriate respect and honor for their faithful labor, but there are no superstars in God's army. There are only soldiers laying down their lives for the Master. Many a young man settles into his first post aspiring to join the greats, but he and they will be better served if he remembers 1 Corinthians 3:7. 'For neither he who plants nor he who waters is anything, but only God who gives the growth'.

Second, you are God's gift to your church. It's not a typo. The distinction between these first two is very

129

important. American celebrity culture has invaded evangelical churches. We've moved well past appreciating the extraordinary gifts of some preachers and teachers to cult-like hero worship and a gross lack of perspective. Technology provides access to voluminous audio and video resources giving unprecedented access to our 'favorite' preachers. While we should rejoice that believers are feasting on the Word during the week, the practice can fuel unhealthy comparisons and unrealistic expectations. I've been shaped by the preaching ministries of Alistair Begg, John MacArthur, Matt Chandler, David Platt, John Piper, Mark Dever, Steven Lawson, and many more. And if you ask me, I think that they are much better preachers than I am. If given the option, I'd expect every member of our church to prefer one or more of them over me. I say this, not out of self-pity or false humility, but because I believe it's true.

Despite their superior intellect and ability, God didn't send any of them to pastor Parkway Baptist Church. In His infinite wisdom and by His gracious providence, God sent me to labor in this field. To use Paul's words, the 'Lord assigned' this work to me. Therefore, no other man can fulfill this ministry. Even though we might assess their fitness for this field and deem them more suitable for it, God apparently does not agree. This is no ground for pride and arrogance; rather, this truth ought to give each of us a humble confidence to minister faithfully according to the gifts God has given to us.

Third, you're only one in a line of builders. God has given you to your congregation for this moment, but you are not the only pastor they will need. If you're laboring in an established church, this point will be obvious. Men preceded you in that field, and if the Lord tarries, more will follow behind you. Even if you are the founding pastor and planter of your church, the foundation is Jesus and your church did not appear out of nowhere. We could add also that your congregation will need other pastors or elders laboring alongside you to round out the ministry. Finally, I'm confident you want the church to outlive you. Despite the circumstances of your ministry assignment, you are not sufficient for that congregation's past, present, or future pastoral needs. God will send men to minister before, beside, and behind you.

Paul's writing in this passage clarifies that he knew he wasn't sufficient for God's people in Corinth. He was only building on the foundation of Jesus and others, like Apollos, were necessary cogs in the ministry wheel. The principle is not limited to Corinth. The Church at Ephesus needed more than Timothy. The Metropolitan Tabernacle has outlived Spurgeon's ministry. Grace Community Church will surely not fold when MacArthur hangs it up. By God's grace, your church will outlive you. So take a long view of God's work among your people and take up the mantle that has been entrusted to you. Carry it for as long as God gives it to you then hand it graciously to the next man.

Fourth, you're responsible to build for eternity. Regardless of outward appearances, no human can measure the eternal significance of a person's ministry. It's sobering to ponder that the fires of judgment will reveal the truth. Two ministries may look the same to human eyes, only to find out that one is eternally valuable and the other is worthless. The materials list in verse 12 breaks into two categories: those that are purified by fire and those that are destroyed by it. Some work will emerge from the judgment unscathed and elicit a reward for the builder while other work will be consumed.

This passage forms a pertinent warning to all believers and especially to pastors. We must build on the foundation of Jesus. Borrowing from Paul's statements earlier in the letter, we must not veer from preaching the Word of the cross and making known the spiritual things that are only discerned by spiritual people. All listeners may not grasp it or appreciate it, but, brothers, we must keep our hands on the plough and build for eternity.

Fifth, the Church is God's and He loves her more than you. Paul closes this passage with a warning, which yields a corresponding promise. The church is God's. He loves her. He sent His Son to die for her. He has given His Spirit to dwell in her. He will build her and protect her. He will bring her all the way home. Ultimately, He will exact vengeance on those who harm her and reward those who sacrifice for her. I pray we will grow in our enjoyment of and affection for the congregations we serve, but we will never outdo God in loving these sheep. He is committed to their ultimate good, He has begun a good work in her, and He will bring it to completion on the last Day (Phil. 1:6).

Therefore, follow Him in how you lead, feed, protect, and care for your congregation. Remain committed to their ultimate good. Don't let them settle for less than God's best. Give them the substance of God's Word and not the candy of spiritual pep-talks. Don't trade the eternal reward of faithful labor for the momentary applause of popularity. Be patient with these sheep. Love them when they don't appreciate what you're trying to do. Brothers, persevere in this work.

8

PREACHING THROUGH ADVERSITY

I suspect most everyone has one in some form or another. For more than twenty years of marriage, my wife and I (James) have always maintained ours in a kitchen drawer. It's conveniently located for easy access in the hub of our home. The drawer isn't nearly big enough, so items routinely fall out the back onto the pots and pans below. It's the place for random stuff that you need regularly (or randomly) but don't want out in the wide open and visible. Our junk drawer has a few staples: pens and pencils, at least one sharpie marker, a notepad, a rubber band or two, some paper clips, our church directory, appliance manuals, a couple of small screwdrivers, a pair of scissors, and a razor blade.

In addition to these basics, you're likely to find just about anything in there that will fit (or almost fit) into the drawer. Batteries have been known to hang out there for months, but you probably won't find one there if you really need it. I've been stuck by the sharp end of a thumbtack reaching in for a pen more than once, so I'm not a fan of keeping those in there. I'm fairly certain we kept an out-of-use garage door opener in that drawer for upwards of a year at one point. You're going to need this stuff at some point, and when you do, it should be close at hand. Thus, you should cram it in that drawer and shuffle it around in search of the small flathead screwdriver for months on end.

You can hear the frustration, but this drawer is a reasonable solution for keeping up with the odds and ends of daily living. Whatever your solution, surely you have a comparable catch-all place in your home. Similarly, we're using the word *adversity* as something of a catch-all category. Aside from overt hostility and wearisome apathy within the church, the preacher faces a host of struggles and trials that threaten his resolve to endure in the preaching ministry. While few men face every form of adversity, all of us face a mountain of it. Thus, we have compiled several examples from our ministries here to put a twenty-first century face on what most of us know all too well.

Meanwhile, Back in Corinth

Before delving into our stories, let's go back to Corinth. Based on a careful reading of the two New Testament letters from Paul to these believers, it's clear he wrote at least two more that are not preserved in the Canon. Without wading into the scholarly debate, we hold that 1 Corinthians is the second letter and 2 Corinthians is the fourth. Drawing from them and using the narrative of Acts to fill-in the story, we understand the depth and difficulty of the relationship between this congregation and her founding pastor. This final correspondence provides a protracted defense of himself and his ministry with brutal honesty and surprising hope. He shares something of a ministry memoir complete with vivid descriptions of obstacles and trials while contending that through this suffering he is ever encouraged and joyful.

This letter is a gift to the Church through the inspiration of the Spirit and it is a special treasure to pastors. As Barnett notes, it 'is a rich lode for the edification of God's people' containing 'many inspiring texts and passages to the .... teacher of God's Word.'[1] Alongside the Pastoral Epistles, this letter contains directed instructions for pastors, particularly in the realm of endurance and patience, that 'stand as a model and an inspiration to subsequent generations.'[2] From the opening benediction to the stirring testimony of God's sufficient grace in Chapter 12, this letter forefronts Paul's suffering as the means God is using to display His glory through His apostolic ministry.

After giving a survey of his relationship to this church in the first chapter and a half, Paul defends his ministry from the middle of Chapter 2 through to the first verses of Chapter 4. This defense bleeds into broader statements about perseverance that continue through this chapter. We pick up that theme to offer specific encouragement for pastors laboring in the pulpit through tremendous adversity. Paul makes the same statement to bookend this section: 'we do not lose heart.' Despite the indicative nature of the text, it functions imperatively for those, like

---

1. Paul Barnett, 'The Second Epistle to the Corinthians' in *New International Commentary on the New Testament* (Grand Rapids, Eerdmans, 1997), 47.

2. Ibid., 50.

Paul, who serve the church as pastors and missionaries. We mustn't lose heart either.

We land here to make this plea not only because it's a straightforward call to endurance, but because this passage puts adversity forward as a gift to the preacher and his congregation. God is not merely allowing suffering; He brings it for the good of His servants and for the sake of His glory. Adversity is not an enemy to be destroyed; it is a gift to be embraced. In one of the strange paradoxes of the Christian faith, Paul argues that death is life-producing. This life, which is found in the 'light of the knowledge of the glory of God in the face of Jesus', shines through the disposable, common, breakable, ordinary jars of human instruments. And this light is most clearly seen and appreciated when the jar is shown to be utterly weak yet unexplainably persistent.

Paul's attitude toward suffering is perspective-shaping and immanently helpful. One key to enduring through adversity is to embrace it as a sweet gift delivered by the sovereign and gracious hand of God. More on that in a moment, but first, let's go back to Kentucky.

Now Back to Kentucky

Some churches and pastors carry a disproportionately heavy burden. The crises and tragedies in some fields seem exorbitant. We look back over years of ministry in our respective places in full realization that the seasons of blessings and moments of joy far outweigh the times of adversity. We provide these anecdotes to give present tense to the timeless theological truths of 2 Corinthians 4, but neither of us would contend that our suffering is exceptional or especially noteworthy. We are ordinary men, serving in ordinary fields, facing ordinary adversity. Reflecting on the categories of crises Spurgeon faced, as shown previously, we offer a few examples.

When it comes to public criticism and ridicule, relatively few men know what it's like to have disparaging newspaper articles written about them. Yet, most of us have caught the swirling wind of criticism aimed at us. I know this first hand (Brian). I mentioned earlier the mass exodus of the pastoral committee that hired me, in large part because of my preaching. One of those committee members left making a lot of noise. She not only hated my preaching, but she grew hostile towards me over a couple of decisions I made that she didn't like. This led her to slander me and go out of her way to seek out other pastors to tell them how much she despised me. She then rallied her friends and family to help. Some of the things she said were true and were decisions I made that she didn't like. I can live with those things.

The slander, the lies, and the blatant efforts to mar my reputation around the community with untrue stories were much more difficult to endure. I remember walking into a community coffee shop and people who had never met me knew me because of this well-connected women's demolition efforts to take me down. Similar experiences happened at the grocery store, bank, and funeral homes. Her family knew a lot of people and wanted me to know it.

Fighting outside the church is tough, but when the adversity invades the home it often takes on a greater intensity. These struggles might seem insignificant to others, but we'd liken them to surgery. As the saying goes, 'the only minor surgery is the one someone else is having.' Here are a few examples of adversity in our homes.

No Place to Live

The fall of 2013 was a roller coaster for our family (James). I was returning from a meeting of pastors in Nashville on a Wednesday afternoon in August when I received a call from a mentor and friend. He wanted to talk because he had just finished eating lunch with the chairman of a pastoral search committee during which they invested a significant portion of the time watching one of my sermons. 'I would love to give them your résumé,' he said, 'but I need you to consider it and determine if God is leading you in this direction.' I made no commitment, except that I would speak to my wife about it when I arrived home. She was neither impressed nor excited. I thank the Lord for her in so many ways and, in this case, for her immediate clarity on the ridiculous nature of that notion. I only entertained this opportunity as an escape hatch and not because God was moving me toward it.

We put that 'opportunity' to rest within forty-eight hours and returned to normal life only to learn about a week later that we would indeed be moving in the next few months. We had been renting a house from a church member for three years and, due to circumstances beyond her control, she needed us to vacate it. We appreciated her grace, sensed her agony, and felt for her. To this day, she's a dear friend and a member of our church. There was no ill-will, but the situation created a crisis for us. We weren't leaving Bardstown, but we were moving. Complicating matters, however, was the fact that we still owned a home in Georgia. The housing market crash of 2009 eliminated the equity in our home forcing us to hold onto it and rent it out when we came to Kentucky in 2010. The prospects of buying a second home were bleak, but we quickly learned that the rental market yielded few options that fit our price range and needs.

For about five weeks, we scoured the market for available places and grew more anxious by the moment. At some point along the way, we determined it would be cheaper each month to pay a mortgage than to pay rent and focused our energies in that direction. In late September, we put down an offer on a house and negotiated for a few days haggling over a couple of thousand dollars. The seller left town for a long weekend on a scheduled trip and we expected to close the deal without any problems when he returned. Relieved, we spent the weekend mentally decorating the home and making plans. The call from our realtor on Monday morning rattled me more than I'd like to admit. After receiving zero offers in eleven months, the seller received an offer higher than ours over the weekend and had accepted it. He provided no opportunity for us to counter. The deal was done, the house was sold, and we were back to square one.

To increase the tension, I was scheduled to leave the country that Saturday for Haiti. We discussed the wisdom of my going, given the uncertainty of our situation, but decided I should keep the commitment. I boarded a plane on the last Saturday in September knowing that we would move before the end of October, but uncertain as to where we would go. The stress of the situation was great, but it did not compare to the inner strife produced by that eight-week period. The possible opportunity to leave, the failed attempt to buy a home, and the inability to find a place to go combined to create a burden that brought me to the brink of despair.

It may not seem like much in one way, but the threat of homelessness exposed the dangerous mirage of self-sufficiency in my heart and mind. Because my instincts seemed wrong at every turn, I began to doubt myself and wonder about God's care and control. The Lord's kindness showed powerfully in the weeks that followed. Not only did He provide abundantly for our physical needs, He sanctified me in the process. He exposed the absurdity of my self-sufficiency and proved His steadfast loyalty. It didn't feel like it at the moment, but that adversity was a gift.

Identity Crisis

I hit a horrible wall about ten years into my ministry at my church (Brian). It was in a season where my ministry in all areas was flourishing. But my soul was dying. My marriage was struggling. My wife was in a dark place. I had run our family into the ground and had done the same to myself. So much of the mental and emotional breakdown I experienced was rooted in ministry becoming my identity. And I was terrified to face it. It took almost losing it all for me to get help. Even then I did it begrudgingly. God used a very wise and skilled counselor and some close, patient pastoral friends to take me on a journey long needed. It was a very painful journey that shook my identity to the core and that began with seeing the reality of my weakness and humanity.

At my lowest moments I struggled to get out of bed in the mornings. My joy was gone, and it was a challenge to even accomplish my daily responsibilities. It was a journey to understand and embrace my weakness and trusting Jesus would meet me there – and give me strength. He did.

I am still on this journey, but my life is radically different. My soul is at peace in a way I never thought possible. I have experienced firsthand that, in Christ, there is indeed strength when we embrace our weakness (2 Cor. 12:9-10). This identity crisis and adversity that almost cost me my ministry and family was an incredible gift from God that reshaped and reset the trajectory of them both. In the midst of it all, God was still building his church among us. It didn't feel like it at the moment, but that adversity was a gift.

Seizures and Slander

Everything seemed to be humming along smoothly for us (James) as we neared the end of school in 2015. I first noticed something strange was happening with my son as we tossed baseball in the backyard. Every now and then, he'd lose focus. All of a sudden, he'd drift mentally and completely disengage with what was happening all around him for ten to fifteen seconds. At first, we shrugged it off as child-like daydreaming. He's the type of kid who can shut out the world when he concentrates, so we thought he was just hyper-focusing at inopportune times.

The situation continued to intensify, however, and we grew convinced that he might be suffering from a medical illness. Our pediatrician and personal friend advised us to keep an eye on him to note exactly what was happening and schedule an appointment in a week or so. That space of time was important for us to monitor him closely and it was excruciating as we watched him suffer through those periods. After a brief medical exam, the doctor made an initial diagnosis that shocked and scared us. While he referred us for neurological testing to confirm it, his opinion was that our son had a form of epilepsy and that he was suffering from absence seizures. Within a week, further testing and consultation from the neurologist confirmed it and our son started taking medication. As others whose children have faced illness and disease will know, the ground beneath us was not stable. In the grand scheme of medical possibilities, this diagnosis could have been much worse, but the weight of that struggle was indescribable.

By God's providence, the day I took my son to his appointment with the pediatrician, I was called into another meeting. A member of our church had contacted the office to ask about a letter she received in the mail that day. The typed, anonymous letter was a slanderous attempt to discredit me personally and disparage my ministry. With an unknown number of letters circulating, a few of our leaders wanted me to know about it and express their support. That week, which included a sleep-deprived EEG for my son, also included leadership meetings to discuss the veracity of the letter and the appropriate response. The ministry burden couldn't compare to my concern for my son, but it added to the size of the trial.

God's provision and care for us during that week was extraordinary. When we look back, we can see how He was planning for and orchestrating events to care for us more than two decades prior. The letter is a distant memory and my son, by God's grace, has not had another seizure since the Monday that followed that first appointment with the pediatrician. It didn't feel like it at the moment, but that adversity was a gift.

Matters of the Heart

At the height of the conflict while trying to survive the third firing attempt in five years, I had a health scare (Brian). I started to have anxiety attacks as well as heart palpitations. When they got bad it was scary because they would take my breath away for a moment. They got bad enough where I eventually had to go to the doctor to run some tests. They hooked me up to a heart monitor so they could observe what was happening.

Ironically, my doctor made an observation as he sought to find what was wrong as he casually asked: 'So, how much stress are you under?' I was a bit taken aback by his question, so I responded, 'Well, about as much as everyone else who is pastoring a church and has a young family, I guess,' downplaying the hostile church environment I had lived in for the last half decade. Then he asked something that God used in a powerful way: 'Did you know most research agrees you have one of the most stressful professions anyone can have?'

That was the first moment the dots began to connect. The stress from the last five years could be the cause of my heart issues. I was the classic example of the frog in boiling water and I had missed the connection. Not anymore. I began to care for myself in a different way. I started taking all my vacation time. I realized I had limitations and I needed to listen to them if I wanted to be able to do this well into the future. I started listening to my body to grow in awareness of the emotional and mental stress in my life. It didn't feel like it at the moment, but the adversity caused by the hostile church environment was a gift.

Seasons of Sorrow

The final example of adversity for me (James) to share comes with no story. It is not an event and cannot be captured as one episode. I would describe it as despondency. It seems to be much less than what is often called depression and yet more than simple discouragement. It's not an overwhelming sadness, but a recurring melancholy that erodes my joy. Certainly, circumstances play a role, but are not the over-riding cause in all cases.

The struggle is not constant, but it is persistent enough. It comes like a fog to encompass my heart and mind, at times without warning. When a day or a moment seems bright and my heart is resting content in God, a hint of fear or dread will invade to capture my attention. Then the encircling density of sorrow will weigh on me. Unfortunately, I have learned to compensate for it in moments of ministry, and to most I appear mostly normal. But deep within, an ache of gloom casts an ominous shadow over my soul.

In these moments, delight feels just out of reach. This cloud of darkness is not unbearable in one sense, but the lingering nature of it wearies my spirit. As I wrote to my wife recently about it, 'I'm tired of being so frail and unstable. I'm tired of pouting and complaining about it. I'm tired of wallowing in self-pity and inwardly moping again every few months.' The combination of my inadequacies and failures within and problems and pressures without form an abundant concoction of despair.

In the midst of this adversity from the inside, I'm tempted to sin in two specific ways. First, I attempt to 'grit and go' by powering through in human strength. Second, I contemplate an escape. Not an escape from life itself but one from the lot I've been given in pastoral ministry. God is graciously sustaining me. Brothers, some will battle with depression and need the common grace of medicine and medical care. Others can speak with greater expertise, but please do not forsake these potential instruments in the name of spirituality.[3] For many, however, the adversity of spiritual sorrow is something of a recurring moment of realization that all in the world is not right. It leaves us slumping and despondent. If this describes you, do not despair, you're not alone. It won't feel like it in the moment, but even this adversity is a gift.

Encouragement for Enduring through Adversity

Our stories are unique in one sense and ordinary in another. We're not the first or the last to struggle with conflict, crises, illness, and despondency, but our particular trials are deeply personal. Every pastor could write his own chapter, and some could write an entire book. Once again, our heart is neither to trumpet ourselves as exemplary sufferers nor to wallow in self-pity. We have been, by any sensible account, graciously and abundantly blessed. But persevering is never easy. Whether your list is longer or shorter than ours, you will not endure it without the ministry of the Spirit through the Word in your life. That's our aim as we close this chapter.

---

3. For anyone struggling with overwhelming discouragement, we recommend you seek the ministry of a Certified Biblical Counselor. Find one near you at biblicalcounseling.com.

Read again 2 Corinthians 4 and note Paul's transition from a defense of his ministry to an explanation of why and how he perseveres in hardship. Also, pay careful attention to the clear inference that adversity, while excruciating in the present, is a gift from God.

Therefore, having this ministry by the mercy of God, we do not lose heart. But we have renounced disgraceful, underhanded ways. We refuse to practice cunning or to tamper with God's word, but by the open statement of the truth we would commend ourselves to everyone's conscience in the sight of God. And even if our gospel is veiled, it is veiled to those who are perishing. In their case the god of this world has blinded the minds of the unbelievers, to keep them from seeing the light of the gospel of the glory of Christ, who is the image of God. For what we proclaim is not ourselves, but Jesus Christ as Lord, with ourselves as your servants for Jesus' sake. For God, who said, 'Let light shine out of darkness,' has shone in our hearts to give the light of the knowledge of the glory of God in the face of Jesus Christ.

But we have this treasure in jars of clay, to show that the surpassing power belongs to God and not to us. We are afflicted in every way, but not crushed; perplexed, but not driven to despair; persecuted, but not forsaken; struck down, but not destroyed; always carrying in the body the death of Jesus, so that the life of Jesus may also be manifested in our bodies. For we who live are always being given over to death for Jesus' sake, so that the life of Jesus also may be manifested in our mortal flesh. So death is at work in us, but life in you.

Since we have the same spirit of faith according to what has been written, 'I believed, and so I spoke,' we also believe, and so we also speak, knowing that he who raised the Lord Jesus will raise us also with Jesus and bring us with you into his presence. For it is all for your sake, so that as grace extends to more and more people it may increase thanksgiving, to the glory of God.

So we do not lose heart. Though our outer self is wasting away, our inner self is being renewed day by day. For this light momentary affliction is preparing for us an eternal weight of glory beyond all comparison, as we look not to the things that are seen but to the things that are unseen. For the things that are seen are transient, but the things that are unseen are eternal.

Adversity is a gift to remind us that we are insufficient for this work. God never intended for the containers to rival the beauty of what they hold. He didn't design the conduit to outshine the content. To eliminate any doubt about where the power in gospel ministry resides, He uses adversity to demonstrate it. Paul lists four specific varieties of adversity in verses 7 and 8: affliction, confusion, persecution, and physical assaults.

In every case, the significance is not the suffering itself, but the fact that suffering does not win. Each participle of suffering is contrasted with another participle of negation. Our affliction does not leave us trapped. Our confusion does not leave us in despair. Our persecution does not leave us without God. Our physical beatings do not destroy us. Indeed, these will push us to the brink of our capacity, but the God who sends them is the God who sustains us. We are not capable for this charge. We are not strong enough or smart enough and adversity is a gift to serve as an intimate reminder of our utter dependence on God. Therefore, embrace it.

Adversity is a gift to manifest the life of Jesus through His servants. Without God's sustaining grace, suffering would ruin a man. But, as Paul teaches in verses 10 and 11, they become avenues for the display of the life of Jesus in us. If it's true that we do not live by our own strength, then adversity comes along to prove it. The Greek word *hina* communicates purpose in the middle of verse 10. He refers to suffering as 'carrying in our body the death of Jesus' for the purpose of displaying Jesus' life.

The pastor who appears to be self-sufficient suppresses the shimmer of Jesus' abundant, resurrected life. God intercepts these misguided notions by laying the weight of adversity on His servants and then radiating His life through them. We cannot adequately display the rich life of our resurrected Savior without the dark valleys of suffering that contrast our insufficiency with His absolute sufficiency.

Adversity is a gift to bring life to your congregation. Moving from the display of Jesus' life in the suffering servants of Jesus, Paul explains the reverberating impact on the people of God. Simply stated, when death is at work in the pastor, life is at work in the church. The seedlings of life in the church sprout from the seeds of suffering in the pastor. Verse 12 only reinforces the truth that some of God's work in a congregation has always been mediated through the transforming work He does in the pastor. Our endurance in suffering sends out ripples of God's grace among His people for God's glory.

If you want God's glory to increase through your congregation as they grow in trust, in godliness, in perseverance, in holiness, in peace, in patience, and so on, then we must pass perseveringly through the fires of trial as they watch. In these times, we can give them a present illustration of what it looks like for a believer to walk by the Spirit in any and every circumstance. If you long for the sanctification of your people, then don't despise adversity for it is an instrument in God's hands for their life.

As a downstream application of this truth, adversity in the pastor gives opportunity for the church to grow in love by pressing them to serve and care for him. Modern ideals about pastoral ministry sometimes wrongly communicate that the pastor is ever-ministering to the church and then reaching beyond the church to receive ministry. While we support ministry to pastors from outside the local church,[4] the most common means of grace for helping the struggling pastor arise from the context of congregational life. Brothers, we rob them of the joy of ministering to us when we fail to expose the reality of our struggle to endure.

Adversity is a gift to prepare us for eternity. Paul repeats the theme of this smaller section in verse 16, 'So we do not lose heart' and then adds this final reason to treat adversity as a gift. Trouble draws our gaze away from a preoccupation with the present by creating a longing for what awaits us. All of us are tempted to count and count-on what is tangible. We cling to our bodies, our health, our reputations, and our ministries, but none of these will last. Even though we

---

4. Brian's ministry through Practical Shepherding operates for this purpose. To learn more, visit practicalshepherding.com.

know this to be true, we need the persistent reminders of our frailty and the passing nature of what can be seen. In this light, affliction can be called 'light' and 'momentary', not because it is easy, but because it pales in comparison to the weight and length of eternity.

Yet, adversity does more than merely produce an eternal perspective. According to verse 17, it 'prepares for us an eternal weight of glory.' The suffering is part of God's purpose – His glorious, gracious, end-time purpose – that will be advanced and not thwarted by the suffering of His people. To borrow from the language of Romans 8:28, He is working our adversity together with all things for our ultimate, eternal good. Therefore, adversity is a gift to be embraced.

We could think of no better conclusion to this chapter than an oft-used quote from Charles Spurgeon. Pastors, let this become our confession: 'I dare say the greatest earthly blessing that God can give to any of us is health, with the exception of sickness .... Affliction is the best bit of furniture in my house. It is the best book in a minister's library.'[5]

---

5. Randy Alcorn, *If God is Good: Faith in the Midst of Suffering and Evil* (Colorado Springs: Multnomah, 2009), 416.

Conclusion

God's Grace is Sufficient to Sustain Your Preaching Ministry

'I am *content* with weaknesses, insults, hardships, persecutions, and calamities' (2 Cor. 12:10).

Our goal in writing this book was not merely to give you a boost to survive another Sunday or even make it for a few more years. The goal is to provide an instrument for the Spirit to reinvigorate your soul. We are aiming at more than eking by or drudging through a white-knuckled, man-empowered, joyless ministry. We are called to much more than that. An exclamation point for this book-length exhortation to endurance is found in 2 Corinthians 12:7-10:

> So to keep me from becoming conceited because of the surpassing greatness of the revelations, a thorn was given me in the flesh, a messenger of Satan to harass me, to keep me from becoming conceited. Three times I pleaded with

the Lord about this, that it should leave me. But he said to me, 'My grace is sufficient for you, for my power is made perfect in weakness.' Therefore I will boast all the more gladly of my weaknesses, so that the power of Christ may rest upon me. For the sake of Christ, then, I am content with weaknesses, insults, hardships, persecutions, and calamities. For when I am weak, then I am strong.

As has been emphasized in various places in the book, Paul was not a mentally, physically, or spiritually weak man. He wasn't perfect or super-human, but he was no quitter. This makes his confession regarding the 'thorn in his flesh' all the more striking. The speculation about what the thorn was is an exercise in futility as far as we're concerned. Paul could have easily identified it, but the Spirit withheld that information. Even more, we contend that the ambiguity serves us well to draw attention away from the manifestation of suffering and on to the larger point of the passage. Namely, a true believer will boast in his weakness and not in his apparent strength. The thorn presented a tangible trial for Paul that can be correlated to the various struggles with hostility, apathy, and adversity that every preacher faces. We put forward a threefold, final charge based on his self-reflection and conclusion.

First, *let your suffering cultivate humility in you*. One of the most significant blind-spots for pastors, and especially young pastors, is a lack of self-awareness. Many men don't understand who they are, what their gifts are, or how they are perceived. In absence of this awareness, pride grows in our hearts to the detriment of our souls and our ministries. Paul, too, admits in verse 7 to facing the temptation of pride because of the privileged nature of his apostolic role. The thorn, therefore, was a God-given reminder of his frailty and a defense against pride.

Suffering, in every form, is a grace from God for our sanctification. As we've tried to emphasize throughout this book, hostility, apathy, and adversity are critical instruments for God's work to shape preachers into Christ's image. Our response to them peels back the façade of self-sufficiency we often present exposing hidden seeds of pride and deadly forms of idolatry. If left to germinate and bud, these sins will leave a swath of destruction in our lives and ministries. Therefore, allow suffering to drive you back to the cross of Christ to reflect upon your utter hopelessness and the sufficiency of our hope in Christ. These tender moments of mental and spiritual re-orientation must become an anchor for our souls amidst the swirling winds of suffering. You cannot fulfill this ministry on your own, even given your spiritual gift of preaching and teaching. We are dependent on Him in everything.

Second, *let your suffering cultivate a warrior mentality in you*. It's clear that God was firmly in control of this thorn with complete authority to remove it. And yet, the adversary seizes this opportunity to harass Paul. Satan hates us and our charge to preach the gospel; thus, he longs to see men fall from this work. Once again, Luther warns of this enemy. 'How difficult an occupation preaching is. Indeed, to preach the Word of God is nothing less than to bring upon oneself all the furies of hell and of Satan, and therefore also of ... every power of the world. It is the most dangerous kind of life to throw oneself in the way of Satan's many teeth.'[1]

---

1. Martin Luther as quoted by David Prince 'Lead from the Front: The Priority

The battle we wage is not merely against flesh and blood. The opponent seated in the pew is not the truest enemy. The affliction is not merely physical or even emotional. Our calling is a forward attack on a bitter and angry foe. This book is not merely some wisdom for life, it's a call to arms. Fight every day in the moments no one sees by feasting on the riches of His Word, communing with Him in prayer, and practicing spiritual disciplines for the purpose of godliness.[2] Remember to read the Word slowly to soak in nourishment for your soul and not just to study for your next sermon. Make your heart and mouth sing of God's mercies more than once a week. Work to memorize God's Word storing it in your mind and hiding it in your heart. Cultivate friendships with unbelievers with an aim for evangelism.

In addition to these disciplines, we exhort you to walk in relationship with other brothers (both pastors and non-pastors) in mutual discipleship. God will pour you out as a drink offering for His glory, but He never intends for you to be empty. Faithful friendship from a few is one of God's kind graces to sustain you. G.K. Chesterton memorably noted: 'There are no words to express the abyss between isolation and having one ally. It may be conceded to the mathematician that four is twice two. But two is not twice one; two is two thousand times one.'[3] In the midst of the difficult labor of leading, feeding, protecting, and caring for

---

of Expository Preaching' in *A Guide to Church Revitalization,* edited by R. Albert Mohler, Jr., (Louisville, KY: SBTS Press; 2015), 32-33.

2. To this end, we have been helped personally and pastorally by Donald Whitney's excellent work, *Spiritual Disciplines for the Christian Life.*

3. G.K. Chesterton, *The Man Who Was Thursday: A Nightmare.* Accessed on 10-29-18 http://www.gutenberg.org/ebooks/1695.

the flock of God, persist in the basics of training yourself for godliness. Let our peculiar suffering – hostility, apathy, and adversity – drive us continually to fight for joy through these ordinary means of grace.

Third, *let your suffering cultivate contentment in you.* That word, content, leaps off the page when I read this passage. Most days Paul's words in verse 10 seem like an impossibility. Contentment in hostility, apathy, and adversity appears at first blush to be somewhere between naiveté and masochism. But Paul gives the ground for our contentment in the surrounding statements. Our satisfaction and even delight in suffering, he argues, grows out of an awareness that weakness is the platform for the display of Christ's strength. The sufficiency of God's grace and the perfection of His power are revealed in the depths of our trial.

Therefore, we endure these trials gladly because through them the power of Christ rests on us for the sake of His Name. The cause of Christ is furthered by the pouring out of His men as an offering of sacrifice before His people. We close with the sobering and inspiring words of a little-known twentieth century Presbyterian preacher, Bruce Thielemann:

> [T]hose anointed to it as the sea calls its sailors; and just like the sea, it batters and bruises and does not rest .... To preach, to really preach, is to die naked a little at a time, and to know each time you do it that you must do it again. Only one certainty sustains the preacher: That God never denies a man peace except to give him glory.[4]

---

4. Mike Bullmore, '7 Things I've Learned about Preaching (Part 2),' accessed 10-25-18 https://www.preachingtoday.com/skills/2014/september/seven-things-ive-learned-about-preaching-part-2.html.

ACKNOWLEDGEMENTS

James:

God has been so gracious to surround me in this project and in ministry with His grace in the form of others. Some have helped with the writing part and all are helping with the persevering part. At the top of that list are the three people with whom I share a home: my wife, Mikila, and our children, Kenna and Jake. I'm grateful for their sacrifices and prodding during the writing process. I pray they grow to love Christ and His Bride more and more as God sustains me to persevere through the snarls and scowls of pastoral ministry.

This book would never come into print without my friend and co-author, Brian. Thanks for sharing your story with me, listening to my idea, and persevering with me in this project. I continue to be blessed by our friendship and partnership in the gospel.

To my brothers and sisters at Parkway Baptist Church, thank you. I pray those who read this book will not draw the mistaken conclusion that serving as your pastor is anything less than a true joy. Those of you who have encouraged me in specific ways over these last eight years far outnumber the critics. God is using you, your kind words, and, most importantly, your prayers to stabilize and strengthen me. I'm thankful for our leadership teams – staff, elders, deacons, and administrative team – that support me and are persevering with me in this field. Every ministry field has challenges and this one is no exception, but I love you all and I love serving you.

Finally, a few of my friends deserve thanks for helping to bring this book to reality. I'm grateful for a few men who are walking most closely beside me during this season: Mr. Stan, Josh, Jacob, Mike, Eric, James, and Corey. God is using you to re-form my heart and re-shape my life. Thank you. To the faithful band of readers and editors – Randall, Ed, and Marshall – thanks for making significant contributions to the final product.

Brian:

Randall Cofield has been a sweet partner in ministry and a treasured friend these last few years. Thank you, brother, for serving us with your thoughts and edits to this work that made it much better.

Ryan, Jim, and Rob, thank you dear brothers for your meaningful friendship, steadfast example, and for teaching me much of what is in this book.

Without my congregation, Auburndale Baptist Church, this book becomes an exercise in theory and objective principles. Instead, you have made this book deeply personal and redemptive. It is one of the great joys of my life to be your pastor and to have walked this journey with you.

My family lived through every moment of my ministerial adversity. It is impossible to measure how much God used my wife, Cara, and my children, Samuel, Abby, Isabelle, and Claire to encourage me and urge me to press on. This is not my story, but ours. Thank you for your love and steadfast support of me.

Brian and James would like to also thank ...
Willie Mackenzie and Christian Focus for your partnership with us and Practical Shepherding. We love working with you!

The Board of Practical Shepherding for your support, friendships, and encouragement of this project.

The Great Shepherd of the sheep, Jesus, who gives us a small glimpse of the glory of His Bride. We are grateful to be beloved by you and included in this important work to redeem your church.